FLYING ON A WING AND A PRAYER

The second glider managed to clear the trees and flared out close to the ground; just as it touched the ground it found a hidden obstruction, lurched violently around and slid backward along the ground with one of its wings broken and twisted. It came to a halt resting on its good wing but facing in the direction it had just come.

By now, John Alison had discovered that the glider carrying the temporary runway lights and "airport" control equipment was missing and he quickly set about improvising some form of lighting system. As he started to exchange existing smudge lights, another pair of gliders came down into the confusion. One of the pilots managed to use the last of his flying speed to lift his craft over a wrecked glider and he landed roughly, but safely, beyond it. The pilot of the second glider obviously did not see the wreck—he flew straight into it at about ninety miles an hour. When the terrible crashing noise stopped, the nightmare screams of the wounded filled the clearing. Again, medics raced to help, but most of the men were to lose their lives. . . .

Bantam Books in The Fighting Elite™ series

U.S. MARINES
U.S. RANGERS
U.S. NAVY SEALS
U.S. AIR COMMANDO

The Fighting Elite™
U.S. AIR COMMANDO

Ian Padden

BANTAM BOOKS
TORONTO • NEW YORK • LONDON • SYDNEY • AUCKLAND

THE FIGHTING ELITE™: U.S. AIR COMMANDO
A Bantam Book / October 1985

Produced by Bruck Communications, Inc.
157 West 57 Street, New York, NY 10019.

Cover photo courtesy D.A.V.A.
Inside photos courtesy D.A.V.A.

ISBN 0-553-25059-0

Published simultaneously in the United States and Canada

PRINTED IN THE UNITED STATES OF AMERICA

H   0 9 8 7 6 5 4 3 2 1

To Captain James B. Rossi, American Airlines, my friend and a great 'dog fighting' companion.

And to Fenella Corr, a great lady and aviatrix.

ACKNOWLEDGMENTS

To John Alison for his invaluable assistance; to Bob Moist for all his help; to Thomas Baker for answering my innumerable questions; and to the Commanding Officer and all the men and women of the 1st Special Operations Wing of the United States Air Force, Hurlburt Field, Florida, who afforded me their time and assistance and provided me with priceless information and memories that will always be with me.

Ian Padden.

Contents

Foreword

Traditionally, when a war or battle is mentioned most people think of two opposing armies facing each other from opposite sides of a well-defined front line. It is normal to assume that each army is intent upon pushing the other back or destroying it in order to occupy territory.

As a general rule, whenever nations engage in war—whether on land, at sea, or in the air—as long as there is definite separation, or a front line with the opposing forces being in total control of the territory that they occupy, it is called *conventional* warfare.

However, during any conventional war there are often tactical requirements that necessitate raids or excursions behind the enemy's front lines. These are usually carried out for the purpose of disrupting lines of communication and supplies of war matériels, and for gathering intelligence information, rescuing friendly agents or downed pilots, or just simple harassment to confuse the enemy.

This sort of operation falls under the heading of *unconventional*, or special, warfare, and, as well as requiring a very different tactical approach from that of conventional warfare, it requires specialized equipment and uniquely trained personnel.

Another form of unconventional warfare—perhaps the most modern of all—that has become prevalent in the past twenty years is that of insurgency. Insurgency exploits the political, social, and economic difficulties of a country in order to create strife and turmoil within the nation; this exploitation is carried out in order to gain support from the people for the insurgents' particular belief or cause. The methods employed are psychological and extremely subversive in nature, and they work equally well in both the so-called primitive and advanced civilizations. However, success in the primitive nations is usually achieved more rapidly.

Guerrilla warfare is the oldest form of unconventional warfare; it is as old as war itself, and guerrillas were originally employed in conjunction with conventional armies. However, in recent times the guerrilla has taken on a new role—he has become both the violent weapon of insurgency and the physical tool of various revolutionary movements for achieving political power.

During the last twenty years, the rise of insurgency and the success of guerrilla warfare against well trained and well armed conventional armies throughout the world has posed a growing threat to the national objectives of the United States. The impotence of conventional forces to handle both the guerrilla and the insurgent has been clearly demonstrated on numerous occasions in recent years. As a result, the United States government directed our military leaders to organize and train special units, within the existing defense structure, in the disciplines and tactics required to counter the growing threat.

Several special units were already in existence, but they were lacking in both manpower and equipment to be a significant counterforce against all but minor incidents. One such unit was the 1st Special Operations Wing of the United States Air Force, more often referred to by their original name, the *Air Commando*.

Although it takes highly trained and dedicated men to perform the missions assigned to any elite fighting force, the men of the Air Commando and Special Operations Wing must attribute a considerable amount of their elite status to some very special aircraft. Consequently, in this book, the capabilities and functions of the aircraft are considered of equal importance to the men who flew them.

1
BATTLEFIELD LOG:
Chindwin River, Burma—
March 3, 1944

On February 5, 1944, Brigadier Sir Bernard Fergusson led the British 16th Brigade out of the tiny Indian town of Ledo. This was the first Chindit Brigade, the brainchild of the British general Orde Wingate. The famous jungle fighters of the British Army had adopted the name Chindit from the ferocious-looking mythical creature—half-lion, half-bird—that adorned most of the pagodas in Burma.

On that morning in 1944, Fergusson was leading the Chindits on the long trek from India deep into the homeland of the ancestors of their mythical name. Their mission was to wreak havoc behind the Japanese front lines, in conjunction with their American counterparts, the famed "Merrill's Marauders."

When the Chindits left Ledo, a small town in the province of Assam in the far northeastern corner of India, they headed north toward the Dihing River and the Chinese border. Far from the prying eyes of the Japanese informers in Ledo, and well to the north of the enemy front line that stretched along the Burma-India border south of Ledo, the Chindits turned eastward and headed through the rugged Patkai Hills, which were really mountains (some of the peaks were as high as nine thousand feet).

The reasons for the Chindits' initial journey to the north were to avoid the Naga Mountains (the steepest part of the range) and to avoid the heavily reinforced portions of the enemy's front line concentrated to the south of Ledo. Although they occupied Burma, the Japanese did not garrison the border in the northern territories, since they assumed that the natural defenses of the dangerous windswept mountain ranges and the almost impenetrable jungle would be sufficient to deter the Allies. However, they underestimated the determination and resourcefulness of the American and British fighting men.

Once over the Burmese border, the Chindits turned south and moved down from the mountains into the dense bamboo and vine jungles in which they had spent months training to live and fight.

After twenty-six days of marching, crawling, and clawing their way in screaming, bitterly cold winds, up and down mountains almost totally devoid of living creatures, and then hacking their way through a caldron of sweltering bamboo-and-elephant-grass jungle with its festering populace of mosquitoes, snakes, jungle cats, flesh-burrowing leeches, and a host of other repugnant animals, reptiles, and insects, the Chindits arrived at the Chindwin River.

The flamboyant Brigadier Fergusson, a huge, fierce-looking man sporting a monocle and a large handlebar mustache, stood with his hands on his hips looking at the mile-wide river in front of him. He had led his three thousand men through 140 miles of some of the worst mountain and jungle terrain in the world, and they had overcome all obstacles without outside assistance.

But the deep, fast-moving Chindwin River, which now sloshed past the feet of the Chindits, was only the halfway point—another 140 miles of jungle and hills lay ahead before their primary target area would be reached.

The mighty river could not be crossed without power-boats, and Fergusson's men, who had already achieved what they had thought impossible, were now convinced that their fearless leader had finally met his match.

However, the wily brigadier had informed only his most senior officers that he had been promised a little extra help in crossing the Chindwin. As he ordered his men to make camp in the jungle alongside the river, a series of short radio messages were sent to his commanding generals at their headquarters on the airfield at Hailakandi in India.

Colonel Philip Cochran, commanding officer of the United States 1st Air Commando, received one of the messages and gave brief orders to his men. The waiting pilots and air crews went to their machines, two unarmed C-47 cargo transport planes. These craft were affectionately known as "Gooney Birds" to the American fighting men, "Dakotas" to the British soldiers, and DC-3s to most civilians. They were to become the workhorses of the Air Commando in the China/India/Burma theater throughout World War Two, and, because of their versatility and sound flying characteristics, they were to be in service again more than twenty years later, at the hands of Air Commando pilots during the Vietnam War.

As the two C-47s taxied out and lined up on the runway, ground crews ran out and fastened ropes to hooks onto the tails of the aircraft. On the other end of the ropes were two large CG-4 cargo gliders, each crewed by a pilot and copilot. These giant wood-and-steel–framed aircraft were fabric covered and had simple controls and navigation instruments. Communications with the tow aircraft were usually achieved through a telephone line that ran along the tow cable, although radios were sometimes used.

The gliders resembled huge boxes with wings and tail sections attached—which was basically what they were—and they had simple fixed landing wheels in conjunction with wooden skis or skids.

The two gliders now sitting at the end of the Hailakandi runway were filled with assault boats, complete with engines. The intention was to land the gliders on the shingle beach in front of Fergusson's men on the banks of the Chindwin River. Once the boats were unloaded, the gliders would be snatched back into the air by the planes that had towed them from Hailakandi. The Chindits, with their pack mules and supplies, would then cross the river and either hide or destroy the boats when they had finished with them.

The first C-47 started to move forward slowly as the pilot eased open the throttles on the two 1,200-horsepower engines. Dust flew back along the dirt strip toward the snub-nosed glider, and the 300-foot-long tow rope stretched taut. The glider pilot telephoned that the rope was under tension a fraction of a second before he felt the first jerk of the line on his heavy craft, and the C-47 pilot eased the throttles smoothly and steadily forward to full power.

As power was applied to the massive radial engines, blue, white, and orange flames streaked out from the exhaust stacks, and the steady throbbing noise of the idling engines started to build into a roar. The propellers churned up more dirt and dust, which, mixed with the fumes of burning gasoline, swirled back over the glider. As the glider bumped and shuddered over the ground, the tow plane became completely obscured in the swirling dust.

The pilot of the glider could smell the mixture of burned gasoline and dust as he applied all his skill and training to the task of keeping his craft in line behind the tow plane he could no longer see. In the swirling dust he held his craft straight by watching the tow rope attached to the bottom of his craft. As long as the line remained straight in front of him, the situation was under control; when it started to move to the right or the left, he had to straighten it immediately, otherwise the glider would start to slew wildly and quickly develop an oscillation that would force him to release the tow rope in order to prevent the glider from being wrecked.

The glider pilot knew that the C-47 pilot had pushed his throttles to full power almost as soon as his aircraft had started to move. This was the most dangerous part of any glider operation—the tow plane had to get up speed as quickly as possible to ensure that the glider's rudders and ailerons would become effective enough to control the powerless craft. Prior to the building up of speed, the slipstream blast from the tow plane's propellers helped to provide some rudder and aileron control, but until the speed actually built up it was an uncomfortable time for the glider pilot, particularly on the dusty Hailakandi runway.

As the speed increased, the slow bumping and thudding of the glider developed into a rapid drumming sound and the pilot felt his controls become much more responsive. He relaxed a little as the dust started to clear and the tail of his tow plane became visible. Meanwhile, the C-47 pilot was concentrating on keeping his aircraft as straight as possible as he waited patiently for his speed to build up sufficiently for lift-off. He could feel the effect of the "pickle" attached to the tail of his aircraft as he had to work a little harder to hold the lumbering Gooney Bird straight on the runway. (Tow-plane pilots used the code name *pickle,* instead of the word *glider,* in the event that they lost their tow in mid-air and had to send a radio message to inform search crews of its position. If the word *glider* was used in the radio message to indicate a downed craft behind Japanese lines, it would have meant certain disaster for the glider when it landed, since the enemy would have been alerted to its position.)

As his copilot called, "Sixty knots," the C-47 pilot knew that the glider was almost at flying speed and about to lift off the ground, but it would be several moments before his C-47 would have sufficient speed to get airborne. He felt the tail of his machine move a little and the C-47 started to accelerate more quickly—

this was the indication that the glider was airborne—and a fraction of a second later he heard the glider pilot's voice in his earphones confirming what he had just felt.

The glider pilot was relieved that the drumming sound of the ground reverberating through the wheels and frame of his craft had now been replaced by the sound of air rushing over his engineless machine. He was now in control of a flying aircraft, but he was not free to do as he wished. He must now keep the glider as close to the ground as possible, since his tow plane had not reached flying speed and was still bouncing along the runway. If he let his glider start to climb, he would lift the tail of the C-47 into the air and cause it to crash—he had seen it happen, and had then watched in horror as the helpless glider that had caused the accident collided with the wreckage of the tow plane. It was a very unpleasant but sobering memory.

Despite the buffeting his glider was suffering from the propeller slipstream, he held his craft in line until the tow plane lifted off the runway. As the C-47 climbed, he continued to hold the glider down until the slipstream buffeting stopped, then he slowly eased back the control column and allowed the craft to rise with the C-47. He would now keep his craft directly behind and below the tail of the C-47, in what was called the "low position."

In this position the glider was out of the "invisible wake,"—the direct slipstream and turbulence created by the C-47's propellers—and it would ride smoothly with no exhaust fumes blowing back into the cockpit. The sound of air rushing over the glider at speeds in excess of one hundred miles per hour would drown out the faint noise of the tow plane's engines as it labored to gain altitude; contrary to what most people think, the noise inside the glider was just as bad as the noise inside the C-47 tow plane.

As the glider pilot watched the wheels of the C-47 slowly retract into its wings he began to relax further—

he knew that the tow-plane pilot would soon start a gentle climbing turn to the left and would continue to circle until sufficient height had been gained to fly over the Patkai Hills and into Burma. As the great metal wing of the C-47 dipped gently to the left, the glider pilot started to concentrate more on the task of keeping his craft in unison with it. This was a serious game of "follow the leader," and it required teamwork. The C-47 pilot would take care to make all his turns as gentle as possible so that the glider pilot would have time to make the corresponding adjustments or corrections. The glider pilot would try to stay in unison, or formation, with the tow plane and not make any turn either tighter or wider than that of the tow plane, as this would start to pull the tail of the C-47 off line and make the C-47 pilot's job more difficult.

The tow-plane pilot would not suddenly increase or decrease power, as this would cause the tow rope to start acting like an elastic band and would leave the glider pilot frantically fighting to stop a vicious jerking and horizontal yo-yo type motion that could easily get out of control. If the jerking became severe, the tow rope could part, and the broken rope would immediately act like a whip and slash through either the glider or the tow plane, or both, depending on the place where the break occurred.

However, it was more likely that the glider would be the recipient of the disaster, as it would be moving into the slashing tow rope, whereas the tow plane was moving away from it. Unfortunately, the rudder and tail section of the tow plane were very vulnerable in a tow-rope failure, and if the jerking seemed to be getting out of hand, the tow pilot would immediately "cut" the glider loose and leave it to its own devices. This would not happen without the glider pilot's being given the opportunity to release the tow from his own end, but he would have only a few seconds, or less, to do it before the tow-plane pilot did it for him.

*   *   *

As the first C-47 and glider started their climbing turn, the second pair were moving down the runway. After almost thirty minutes of climbing, the aircraft were at 8,500 feet—high enough to clear the nearest peaks of the Naga Mountains by about 1,000 feet. The first C-47 Air Commando pilot waited until the second pair of aircraft had climbed up to the same altitude, then the four craft leveled out and set a course for the tiny Burmese village of Singkaling Hkamti, on the Chindwin River.

As they headed steadily east over the hills, both the tow-plane and glider pilots maintained a constant check on each other's navigation. In an emergency, such as an attack by enemy fighters, the gliders would be released and all four unarmed aircraft would have to make the best of a bad situation. Air Commando P-51A fighters were in the air, but they were high above in order to avoid drawing attention to the C-47s and the gliders. If they were called to assist, it would take them some time to reach their unarmed colleagues, and although it might not seem like much help it was at least some comfort to the C-47 pilots. If they could dodge the enemy fighters for five to ten minutes, their fighters would get to them and they stood a chance of surviving.

As for the glider pilots, they were really on their own—they had no option but to find somewhere to land their engineless craft, and that could become a nightmare over the dense Burmese jungle. If they did manage to get their craft down safely they would then have to get away from them as quickly as possible, because the enemy pilots would not leave the gliders in one piece, or anyone alive, if they spotted them. The Japanese pilots had a reputation for shooting at anything that they could not positively identify as their own, and unarmed gliders were ideal targets.

If the glider pilots did manage to survive, the best they could do was either wait for their own search planes, and hope that an enemy patrol did not get to them first, or set out to find a friendly village where they might get assistance in returning to their own lines.

In the middle of Japanese-occupied Burma, staying alive or getting rescued was not easy, but the Air Commando rescue pilots, flying tiny unarmed L-5 aircraft, were as expert as they were daring in their efforts to recover their own pilots, and they were highly successful.

As they approached the Naga peaks, the glider pilot behind the lead aircraft watched in awe as his tow plane suddenly leaped up about a hundred feet; despite the slack he had allowed in the tow cable, there was a vicious jerk on his glider as the rope stretched almost taut. The glider was still shuddering as he pushed the control yoke forward to pick up speed in order to get more slack in the tow rope. He had no sooner done it than he saw the tow plane appear to drop down violently in front of him, but from the sensation that he felt through his body he knew that the tow plane had not dropped. It was the glider that was now moving upward as it encountered the same turbulence that had caught the C-47. For the next twenty minutes both the C-47 and the glider pilots were hurled around in a most erratic manner as their craft were pitched and tossed about in the swirling air currents caused by the mountain range.

There was nothing that could be done about it, there was always turbulence over these mountains, and there were occasions during training flights when it became so bad that the aircraft had to turn back to avoid the possibility of a broken tow rope or serious structural damage to either the C-47 or its pickle.

This flight, however, was not for training purposes—there could be no turning back. The pilots just had to grit their teeth and suffer the unpredictable leaping, sinking, shaking, and shuddering until they cleared the turbulent area.

Although the situation was bad for the C-47 pilots, it

was infinitely worse for the glider pilots. At one point, both glider pilots found themselves accelerated to within about a hundred feet of the tails of their respective tow planes, with the two ropes bowed backward over the gliders' wings. For a few hectic moments the glider pilots struggled desperately to prevent the ropes from becoming tangled and tearing the frail craft to pieces.

They had been suffering the turbulence for about ten minutes when the glider behind the lead C-47 got caught in a sudden, unseen turmoil of swirling air. The pilot and copilot of the second C-47, which was a little distance behind the first pair, watched in horror as the pickle lurched wickedly and suddenly rolled over almost completely on its back. The craft seemed to hang in that position momentarily; the watching pilots were fully expecting to see it plummet toward the mountains below, but then it lurched violently around in a corkscrewlike motion to its upright position.

The pilot and copilot stared at each other, but before they could say anything, their own C-47 started a series of gyrations that forced them to forget everything but the safety of their own craft. For the next few minutes the pilot flew with one hand resting on the red handle marked Emergency Tow Release, and several times came within a split second of pulling it. The lead C-47 pilot had on one occasion started to pull the lever, but, fortunately for his struggling pickle pilot and copilot, he stopped when his C-47 suddenly came back under his control.

In the gliders, the crews were desperately worried about their cargo of boats breaking loose, but they need not have worried—the loading crews had done a good job and the boats were still firmly in place.

When the turbulence finally stopped, the pilots of all four craft were soaked with sweat, despite the much cooler temperatures they were experiencing at eight thousand feet. A few dying shudders of turbulence told them that they were now over the worst, and when they looked down they saw the barren Naga peaks and the Patkai Hills falling astern.

Once over the mountains, the C-47's started a steady descent. The closer they were to the ground, the less chance they stood of being spotted by the enemy, and the ideal height over the jungle, with a pickle in tow, was about one thousand feet. If they had not had pickles behind them, the C-47s would have flown much lower; however, in the event of an emergency cutaway or a broken tow rope, the glider pilot needed at least a thousand feet below him in order to have time to find an emergency landing zone.

As they headed steadily toward the Chindwin River, both tow-plane and glider pilots wondered about the mission. This was the first time that the CG-4A gliders had been in action in Burma, and the craft had been relatively untried before they were shipped from the States.

During training at Hailakandi, the gliders had seemed to function quite well, and their pilots had developed both a reasonable level of skill and a considerable amount of confidence in the craft. There had been stories about the CG-4As being used successfully by Australian troops in New Guinea, but they had landed on long grass fields, not on a sandbar beside a racing river. Still, things had worked out well during training for this mission, and there seemed no reason to think that a good firm sandbar would present too many problems.

From as low as a thousand feet the great Chindwin River was clearly visible to the pilots of the C-47s when they were still twenty miles away from it. The winding Chindwin was of considerable help in navigating, as the pilots were easily able to visibly identify major and minor landmarks and reference points along its length. Accuracy of navigation was important at this point; the pilots could not afford to fly around in search of their target area—their craft were unarmed, and the longer they remained over enemy territory, the greater their chance of discovery by enemy fighters.

As the C-47s approached the river they started a ninety-degree turn to the left. The turn was completed just as the aircraft reached the center of the river; the pilots then flew steadily upstream for almost four miles. It was almost 1800 hours as they neared the sandbar that was the target area. As they approached it, the pilot of the lead C-47 saw the faint, shielded recognition signal from the edge of the jungle. No reply was sent to the signaler on the ground for fear that it might be spotted by the enemy; the tow planes did not falter from their course up the center of the river.

As the glider pilots took a quick look at the sandbar to the right of their craft, the pilots of the C-47s conferred briefly and agreed that the continuous signal from the ground gave the correct call sign and the surface winds for the glider pilots. Brigadier Fergusson's men were watching the aircraft in amazement, and the signaling officer, who had been studying the aircraft through powerful binoculars, advised the brigadier that he had clearly seen the pilots looking directly at the signal lamp. He was convinced that they had made contact.

By now, the rumor was spreading like wildfire through the troops on the ground: the gliders were going to land on the sandbar in front of them and deliver powered assault boats to enable them to cross the river—old "Guts and Garters" Fergusson had done it again!

Their initial delight changed, however, as the aircraft and their trailing gliders droned steadily and unfalteringly by upsteam. The phlegmatic British soldiers began to wonder if the pilots had ever seen them, hidden as they were in the dense jungle, or if it had been a mistake and the aircraft were really just on their way somewhere else. The soldiers had been waiting most of the day for a supply drop of food, medicine, and clothing—mostly clothing, and boots in particular. After weeks of mountaineering and then trudging through the fetid jungles, they were almost down to their bare feet. Boots, at this moment, seemed a lot more important than boats.

About ten minutes after the aircraft and gliders had disappeared upstream, the steady throb of aircraft engines was heard again. The C-47 pilots had, according to plan, continued upriver for several miles without acknowledging the recognition signal. When they were well clear of the Chindits' position, they made another left turn and continued to fly in a wide circle until they arrived back over the Chindwin some three miles downstream from the sandbar. They had dropped down much lower over the river, and as they approached the sandbar, the glider pilots pulled their tow-release handles and took charge of their own destiny. The C-47s then continued steadily upstream as though nothing had happened.

The first glider completed one descending circle; then, at a little over one hundred miles per hour, he leveled out and flew straight onto the sandbar in a near-perfect landing. Chindits raced out of the jungle toward it just as the second glider touched down in a similar manner to the first. The pilots released the latches beneath their cockpits, and the noses of the gliders were lifted upward on their hinges to reveal the assault boats firmly strapped down inside.

Within five minutes the boats were in the water, with their engines running; moments later, filled with the first reconnaissance party of Chindits, they were on their way to the east bank of the Chindwin River. As the glider pilots pulled out their pickup equipment, they explained to the British soldiers what was about to happen. The Tommys gleefully assisted the pilots in rigging up the two "goalposts" and stretching out the two long nylon tow ropes that were attached to the noses of the gliders. The free end of each nylon rope had a large loop in it, which was opened up and suspended between the two poles in the manner of a clothesline.

To the Tommys, this was going to be a show worth watching, and they were quite happy to assist the "crazy" American pilots. They politely inquired as to the mental health of the Air Commando pilots. Were they really going to sit in their machines and wait for the Dakotas to come back and snatch them into the air? The glider pilots said *yes* at least fifty times, and were amazed at how much the British soldiers willingly assisted in rigging up the pickup equipment despite their obvious skepticism and concern.

With both gliders ready for pickup, the Air Commando pilots thanked the Chindits for their help and boarded their aircraft. They heard the drone of the approaching C-47s and saw hundreds of British soldiers lining the edge of the jungle. The soldiers waited in anticipation, and, in the time-honored manner of the warrior breed, the wagers were laid.

The C-47 pilots saw the marker spread out on the sandbar indicating that the gliders and their pilots were ready. They started their descent, with the second C-47 just slightly behind and to one side of the lead craft. A pickup hook trailed behind each C-47 on the end of a wire rope that ran up through the tail of the aircraft and onto the drum of a large winch. When the hook snagged the loop between the poles at the end of the nylon pickup line, the tow rope would start to stretch, approximately twenty percent. This would prevent an initial violent jerk on the glider, which would be accelerated smartly and smoothly into the air. As this was happening, the load on the pickup line would cause the winch inside the C-47 to start paying out against a clutch-type brake. With the wire rope being rapidly fed out from the winch, the stretching nylon tow rope would not run out of "stretch" and cause a severe jerk.

If there was any tendency for the nylon rope to spring back, like an elastic band, when the initial shock load of the stationary glider had been taken, this too would be dampened by the winch paying out the wire rope.

Although this elastic slingshot effect of the nylon rope was at first thought to be a problem, it turned out otherwise, as the combination of the initial stretch of the line and the correct setting of the payout winch completely prevented it from happening.

As the C-47s were starting their pickup run, all hell broke loose. Two strange aircraft came in fast and low from the west and flew right over the tops of the waiting gliders. Assuming that the craft were enemy bombers, the C-47 pilots immediately aborted their pickup attempt. They boosted their engines and headed their unarmed and vulnerable tow planes back to Hailakandi.

Meanwhile, the two "strange" aircraft made a tight turn and came back in over the gliders on a "bomb run"—with clothing, food, and hundreds of pairs of boots. The "enemy" aircraft were the much-needed supply planes, hurrying to provide their needy Chindits before nightfall. Unfortunately, there had been a slight breakdown in communications—the Air Commando had not been told!

Remarkably, the gliders were not damaged by the cargo drop, and the following morning the two suitably humbled C-47 pilots brought their tow planes back along the Chindwin River and fully redeemed themselves by treating the skeptical Chindits to two perfect demonstrations of an air-to-ground glider-recovery operation.

2
HISTORICAL DEVELOPMENT OF THE AIR COMMANDO

The Air Commando is now known only as the Special Operations Wing of the Second Air Division. The name was officially changed on July 8, 1968, during the Vietnam conflict, as it was felt that the name *Special Operations Wing* more truly reflected the function of this elite group.

The history of the Special Operations Wing commenced in World War Two; and, although there were numerous highly efficient Air Force Special Operations groups in operation in all theaters of the war, the most unusual and most visibly successful of them was the 1st Air Commando.

This group was originally formed for the sole purpose of supporting units of the British Army in the jungles of Burma, and it is perhaps due to their remarkable accomplishments that a great number of our military leaders finally recognized the value of aerial special-operations groups. Fortunately, the legacy of the 1st Air Commando is still with us in the form of the Special Operations Wing, although it was almost lost on several occasions during peacetime reorganizations in the Air Force.

*   *   *

The series of events that led to the formation of the 1st Air Commando began on February 8, 1943, when the highly eccentric British general Orde C. Wingate led a mixed force of some three thousand British, Burmese, and Gurkha soldiers, called the 77th Indian Infantry Brigade (there were no Indians in the brigade; it was so named because it was formed in India, a fairly typical British military practice), on a long-range penetration raid from Imphal, India, into the heart of Japanese-occupied Burma.

The Japanese, who believed that they had complete control over Burma, were taken by surprise, and it took them considerable time to organize themselves sufficiently to drive the British out again. The main reason for the delay of the Japanese was confusion—they could not understand what the British were attempting to do. Subsequently, they did not totally commit their forces until they were certain that the fast-moving Chindits were not just a diversionary move for a major assault. This delay allowed Wingate's Chindits time to create a considerable amount of havoc with supply lines and communications before they were eventually driven out of Burma by the determined Japanese.

Wingate was compelled to split up his forces into small groups in order to escape from the enemy. Although some two thousand men eventually escaped into India and China, most were in such poor health that they were unfit for any further combat duty.

Although this "long-range penetration raid" was seen as a success by some, most military leaders in the China/India/Burma theater—both British and American—considered it a disgraceful waste of time and manpower since there had been no practical gains.

British Prime Minister Winston Churchill, however, did not seem to share their view. He saw the raid as a much-needed victory to boost the sagging morale of the war-weary British people, and he exploited it to the fullest extent. The Chindits became instant heroes for their daring raid, and Churchill summoned Wingate to England to hear his personal account of the operation.

When they met in London, Wingate expressed his ideas for further long-range penetration missions into Burma. He suggested that a force of at least twelve thousand men be rapidly positioned far behind the enemy front lines—and this could be achieved only by air transportation. As there were no airfields or suitable landing areas immediately available for such a massive troop deployment, Wingate proposed that a spearhead group of combat troops and airfield-construction engineers, with their equipment, be flown into selected small clearings that could be hastily expanded into sizable airfields.

This spearhead, or airfield-construction group, would consist of some six hundred men, with mules, bulldozers, and all the other equipment necessary to build an airstrip within twelve to sixteen hours. Once this was done, thousands of troops could be flown in quickly to establish a major defensive position, and they could be further reinforced and supplied by air for as long as necessary.

The most difficult part of the operation was to get the engineers and their equipment into the small jungle clearings as quickly as possible. Wingate proposed to accomplish this by using transport gliders, since they were the largest aircraft that could be landed on unprepared ground and in the extremely small clearings.

Churchill, who was at the time under some pressure from President Franklin D. Roosevelt to recapture Burma, was elated by the idea. Although he knew it would not be a full-scale invasion, he saw Wingate's plan as an ideal means of satisfying Roosevelt's demands for an offensive action in Burma. Wingate accompanied Churchill to the Allied Quadrant Conference, held in Quebec, Canada, on August 12, 1943, where he further outlined his ideas to Roosevelt and his Chiefs of Staff.

During Wingate's raid in early 1943, the Chindits had been supplied with food, ammunition, clothing, and water, dropped from Royal Air Force transport aircraft. Wingate and his officers realized that if the aerial resupply and support operations had been more refined, they could have remained in Burma for a much longer period. With this in mind at the Quebec conference, Wingate stressed the need for specialized air-support services.

After much discussion between Roosevelt, Churchill, Wingate, and the Chiefs of Staff, the idea was accepted, and Roosevelt agreed that America would provide the specialized air-support group that Wingate was seeking. Upon Roosevelt's direct instruction, a plan called Project Nine was formulated by General Henry "Hap" Arnold, Commander in Chief of Army Air Forces. The plan would give the Chindits their own private American "air force." Project Nine was classified as top secret and was personally supervised by Arnold in order to ensure its success.

General Arnold realized that he had been given a perfect opportunity to test one of his own pet theories— the total operational support and supply of a ground fighting force by an air force group.

Arnold chose two men to put the plan into operation: Colonel Philip Cochran and Colonel John Alison. They were experienced fighter pilots and were known for their ingenuity, their capacity for work, and their ability to organize.

Arnold outlined to them the complete operational concept: organize and build a small, self-sufficient, independent air force to provide complete operational support for the British Army's forthcoming raid in Burma. The private air force would not be under the control of any existing command structure; it would be controlled directly by Arnold himself. Both men were given the title of Cocommander, Project Nine, and they were given unprecedented authority to recruit personnel and requisition equipment from any organization in the United States Armed Forces.

Philip Cochran and John Alison were ideal men for the task: they had much in common and they were good friends. However, Cochran was more flamboyant than Alison, and it was his character and dashing appearance that eventually immortalized him as Flip Corkin, the air ace, in the cartoon strip "Terry and the Pirates."

Although they were cocommanders and worked in unison at all times, Alison did not like the idea of two commanders. Alison insisted that for practical purposes his friend Cochran—who was senior in rank to him by just two weeks—function as the actual commander of the project while he, Alison, would be deputy commander. General Arnold would not change their titles but he accepted their personal arrangement and dispatched them to build their private air force.

Alison and Cochran, with letters of authority from General Arnold, quickly built their air force. By January of 1944, some six hundred experienced personnel, thirty P-51 fighter aircraft, thirteen C-47 and twelve C-64 transport aircraft, one hundred fifty CG-4 transport gliders, seventy-five TG training gliders, one hundred L-1 and L-5 liaison aircraft, twelve B-25 bombers, and six YR-4 helicopters arrived in India.

The YR-4s were still secret and very few people even knew that such machines existed. However, Philip Cochran had the privilege of seeing the craft during their trials, and when he was assigned to Project Nine he immediately realized their potential for the forthcoming jungle operation. He informed Arnold that he wanted as many as he could have, despite the fact that they were still in the experimental stage.

Arnold ordered that the entire operational inventory of the Army Air Force test center be made available for the project. The machines, and some very surprised test pilots, were shipped to India to make history—this was the first recorded appearance of the helicopter on the battlefield.

*   *   *

The men and equipment for Project Nine, recruited and gathered from almost every theater of operation in the world, were shipped out to the province of Assam, in northeastern India. They were based on two adjoining airfields—Hailakandi and Lalaghat—located just to the south and west of the town of Ledo, near the regional headquarters and training grounds of the British Chindits.

When they first arrived in India they were still operating under the strange title of Project Nine. It was not until March 29, 1944, some three weeks after they had landed the Chindits in the jungle and in the middle of the fighting, that they were assigned the official name 1st Air Commando. Although they shared the airfields with the U.S. Air Transport Command, they did not fall under the same command structure, much to the annoyance of all the regional Air Force commanders.

Even more annoying to the regular Air Force units was the fact that Project Nine had all new equipment and their supplies and spares came directly from the States. In the normal command structure, every unit had to beg and struggle endlessly for spares, new equipment was almost out of the question, and they had to take what was distributed to them from the regional supply depots. A further annoying factor was that the men of Project Nine were obviously elite, or "individualistic," particularly their somewhat flamboyant and dashing commander. They were not exactly misfits, because they did not break the rules, but they did stretch them to their limits.

When they first arrived in India, the men of Project Nine had their complaints, too. One of which was the fact that they did not know who they were, inasmuch as they had no insignia or name designating their group. They were not permitted to use the name Project Nine—that could be used only for official requests and as proof of authority. The lack of an official name or insignia is a lack of identity that traditionally does not rest well with any organization, particularly a military one in a combat environment. As a result, the men decided to do something about it, and it was the transport pilots of Project Nine, specifically Major Thomas Baker, who devised the first unofficial insignia of the Air Commando: a circular white disc with a large black question mark in the center.

The emblem came about because Major Baker and his men felt that since no one, including themselves, knew what the unit's name was, and the question, "Who are we?" was continuously being asked, the ? symbol was appropriate. Shoulder patches and badges were made by a local Indian embroidery store and the ground crews painted the emblem on the tails of their C-47s.

It appears that it was mostly the transport pilots and their aircraft that displayed this emblem. The fighter and bomber pilots did not adopt it, although their aircraft were marked for rapid identification purposes with five large diagonal stripes painted across their fuselages.

There was no official emblem for the 1st Air Commando. Although authorization was requested for one, it was refused, primarily because of opposition from the area commanders of the regular units. They were already upset by the fact that they had absolutely no jurisdiction over the Air Commando, and they insisted that, since it was only a provisional group, it was not entitled to have such a form of recognition. Technically they were correct, and Cochran did not press the issue. However, the men of the Air Commando in Burma had their own ideas, and they chose to ignore the official ruling. They devised and wore an unofficial emblem on their jackets, for "field identification purposes only." The emblem they devised was the official badge of the British Chindits with AIR COMMANDO emblazened over the top. Since the British felt honored at the use of their emblem by their American air-support group, the dissenting area commanders wisely turned a blind eye to its unauthorized use.

Wingate's Chindits, otherwise known as the *Long-Range Penetration Group*, or officially as the 3rd Indian

Division (again no Indians, just West African, Gurkha, and British soldiers), moved into Burma in February and March, 1944. Almost 3,000 marched in from northern India and over 9,000 were airlifted in, using gliders and C-47 aircraft. The airlift was a record-breaking military operation, and that record still stands. In five days, some 9,052 soldiers, approximately 1,400 animals (pack mules, pack ponies, and dogs), and 255 tons of equipment and supplies were landed on jungle airstrips that had been hastily constructed by a three-hundred-man advance party.

However, the most important task was to come when the Chindits spread out to attack the Japanese positions. The success of the operation now depended on the Air Commando and their ability to provide all fighter and bomber support, evacuation of sick and wounded soldiers, and supplies of ammunition, food, and water. Food supplies were essential not only for the men but for the animals, particularly the pack mules and ponies, which could not survive on jungle plants. The dogs, which were used as messengers by the British, also required food, but they generally presented less of a problem than the mules and ponies, since human food could easily fill their requirement.

The lack of drinking water was one of the more serious problems faced by the Chindits, and although there was an abundance of it in the jungle streams and pools, it could be used only by the animals. All water taken from streams and pools had to be either boiled or treated with halazone tablets to sterilize it. Boiling was preferable, but often it was impossible for the fast-moving, fighting Chindits. The halazone tablets had to be allowed to dissolve completely (a slow process), otherwise they were of no use, and sometimes the water was so bad that even when the tablets dissolved they had little or no effect. Water taken from the streams exposed men to amoebic dysentery, schistosomiasis (carried by snails), and a multitude of other dangerous microbes, all of which could cause incapacitation or death.

Phil Cochran devised a method of supplying water to the soldiers: he had the long-range fuel tanks for the fighter aircraft filled with water, and the aircraft would then "bomb" the soldiers with them. Surprisingly, if the tanks were dropped correctly they did not burst, and it proved to be a fast and effective method of supplying water in an emergency situation.

Both British and American records show that the 1st Air Commando fulfilled beyond all expectations the role they were formed for, and, apart from individual decorations, both British and American, they were eventually awarded the coveted Presidential Unit Citation for their actions.

Immediately after the Chindits were landed on the jungle airstrips, Colonel Alison was recalled to Washington by General Arnold. Arnold, elated that the airlift operation had been so successful, had recalled Alison for the purpose of recruiting further personnel for the expansion of the Air Commando in Burma; he had assumed that with the success of the initial operation, the British would now mount a full-scale attempt to recapture Burma.

Alison, who was well liked and respected by the British, knew that they had no intention of retaking Burma, since they felt that the pressure of the U.S. Marines in the Pacific would eventually force the Japanese to withdraw their forces. When he informed Arnold of this, the general was extremely surprised. Neither he nor any of the Chiefs of Staff were aware of this—they had assumed that the British were intent on the recapture of Burma, and Alison had already allocated enough men and equipment to more than double the size of the present Air Commando.

Upon Alison's advice, Arnold had Cochran recalled immediately—such information could not be sent by signal, as secret codes were not entirely trusted. Phil

Cochran, whom the British also trusted, repeated what Alison had said, and Arnold immediately sent him back to Burma.

Alison was then informed that he was to remain in the States to organize and train the 2nd Air Commando, which was later used in both the China/India/Burma theater and in the Pacific. The 3rd Air Commando was also formed; this group saw action in the Pacific theater toward the end of the war.

There were other Air Commando-style operations conducted during World War Two, but they were performed in the name of Special Operations, and they were no less daring or adventurous than the majority of the operations performed by the official Air Commando. In fact, a considerable number of Cochran's pilots were "stolen" from these special-operations groups, and in this book all Air Force Special Operations groups are considered Air Commando as they are more than worthy of the name.

Prior to 1944, small groups of pilots and air crews had been assigned to various Special Operations missions, such as dropping Allied agents behind enemy lines and supplying such agents and various guerrilla groups with arms and equipment. Most of these operations were carried out for the British Special Operations Executive (SOE) and the American Office of Strategic Services (OSS), in conjunction with the Royal Air Force, which had some two years' experience in such operations before the United States entered the war.

One such unit, the 60th Troop Carrier Group, flying C-47s and commanded by Colonel Clarence Galligan, was assigned to the so-called Balkans Air Force. This was a British-controlled unit that supplied Yugoslavian guerrillas with war matériels and training personnel. The Balkans Air Force was a peculiar mixture of British, Americans, Poles, Yugoslavs, Greeks, and Italians, and the 60th Troop Carrier Group was involved in some extremely hazardous mountain and bad-weather flying operations in support of the partisan fighters in the Balkan area.

In March of 1944, General Nathan Twining, commander of the 15th Army Air Force, headquartered in Bari, Italy, gave instructions that a special-operations squadron be formed to assist the OSS and SOE in their operations in southern France and northern Italy. The result of this directive was the formation of the 15th Special Group (provisional) and its first operational unit, the 885th Bomb Squadron (Heavy) Special (the title simple means the 885th heavy-bomber squadron for special operations).

The squadron was first based in Blida, Algeria, and used modified B-17 and B-24 bombers to drop SOE and OSS agents and war matériels behind enemy lines. These heavy bombers were chosen because they had a long-range capacity and could carry tons of supplies. Almost all operations were carried out at night and at low level (five hundred feet); consequently, the aircraft were painted black, and their engines had flame suppressors installed on their exhausts to prevent them from being seen.

Operational control of the squadron was maintained by the Special Projects Operations Center, known as SPOC. It was initially based in Algiers, in the Allied Force Headquarters, and was administered by the SOE and OSS.

Between May and September of 1944 the squadron had flown over eight hundred missions, dropping some 230 agents and almost 1,400 tons of weapons, ammunition, and supplies to agents and partisans. By this time southern Italy was firmly in Allied hands, and the 885th was transferred to Brindisi, Italy, where it was joined by the 859th Bomb Squadron (Heavy), another special-operations group that had previously been based in England.

The two squadrons were in operation until the end of the war, by which time they had flown more than two thousand missions to France, northern Italy, Czechoslovakia, the Balkans, Austria, and even Germany. They had dropped some three hundred agents and over thirty-four hundred tons of weapons, ammunition, food, money, clothing, and medical supplies.

When World War Two ended there was a rapid demobilization of our armed forces and the Air Commando and Special Operations forces were disbanded.

The advent of the Korean War saw an attempt to reactivate the groups in the form of Air Resupply and Communications Wings. The first wing, the 580th, was formed in 1950, and two more, the 581st and the 582nd, were in operation by late 1951. These wings saw limited action in Korea, and by the end of 1953 they had been reduced in size to such an extent that they were virtually ineffectual. By 1956 they had been disbanded.

The main reason for their failure was the lack of support from the Chiefs of Staff, who knew that the Eisenhower administration favored the concept of "Masssive Retaliation" and was indisposed to elite groups and other such unconventional military organizations.

However, the late President John F. Kennedy had the foresight to see the growing problems of guerrilla and insurgency warfare in the modern world. He also realized that conventional military forces were not equipped to deal with it effectively, and he charged our military leaders to prepare and train for such eventualities. Kennedy was acutely aware of the reluctance of senior military leaders to promote any unconventional elitist military group, but by careful handling of the Chiefs of Staff he managed to persuade them to address the problem. As a result, special-forces groups slowly started to grow in the Army and Navy, and the Air Force committed resources to developing its own Special Air Warfare Forces (SAW) to support and assist the other branches. The term *Special Air Warfare Forces* was a generalization. It was used to denote activity in the air-related requirements for counterinsurgency (COIN), psychological operations (PSYOPS), and unconventional warfare (UW).

The first step to resurrect special operations was taken in March of 1961 by General Curtis E. LeMay, Chief of Staff, USAF, when he ordered the formation of the 4400th Combat Crew Training Squadron so that the Air Force would be able to provide a counterinsurgency assistance unit. The first aircraft supplied to the 4400th Combat Crew Training Command were sixteen C-47 transports, eight B-26 bombers, and eight single-engine, two-seat T-28 training aircraft.

In September, 1961, the 4400th was sent on its first mission, code-named "Sandy Beach." A detachment of two C-47s and seventeen men were sent to assist the U.S. Army in training native soldiers in the small West African country of Mali.

On October 11, 1961, Detachment 2A, which consisted of eight T-28s, four C-47s, and eight B-26s, were sent to Bienhoa Air Base, Republic of Vietnam. Their mission was code-named "Farm Gate" and they were to become the first U.S. Air Force unit to enter combat in the Vietnam War.

In April, 1962, with the war in Vietnam escalating, the Air Force was compelled to increase its special-operations capability. General LeMay ordered the formation of the Special Air Warfare Center, and the 1st Air Commando group was reactivated as the fighting, or tactical, unit of the new organization. With the new organizational structure, the 4400th Combat Crew Training Squadron no longer operated as an independent unit; it became part of the reactivated 1st Air Commando.

As the war in Vietnam further escalated, so too did the size and scope of the special-operations forces, particularly the 1st Air Commando group. Within a short time it had become the 14th Air Commando Wing with five squadrons. Two were strike squadrons, which utilized fighter-bomber–type aircraft and an assortment of other heavily armed aircraft; two were psychological-warfare units that dropped propaganda leaflets and broadcast recorded messages over the villages and jungle areas; and one was an all-helicopter squadron engaged primarily in civic-action programs, such as airlifting food and medical teams into native villages and conducting evacuations.

Not all Air Commando squadrons were sent to Vietnam—some were placed in the Panama Canal Zone, Thailand, Africa, and Europe, and they were for the discretionary use of the various regional military commanders.

Vietnam, however, was a battle zone, and it had the greatest operational demand as well as the highest degree of risk. But the Air Commando was again proving that their unconventional methods were effective. By 1965 the 1st Air Commando Squadron, one of the strike units, became the first U.S. Air Force unit to be awarded the Presidential Unit Citation since Korea. The citation commended the unit for its superb performance under some of the most adverse conditions of the war.

Throughout the war in Vietnam the Air Commando special operations units were used for almost every job imaginable in support of both U.S. and Republic of Vietnam troops. A considerable number of their missions were classified as top secret, and information concerning some of them is still highly classified.

In 1968, the name Air Commando was replaced by the name Special Operations Wing, but it did not change the role of this elite group.

When the Vietnam War ended, the wing was reduced in size for peacetime operations. Further gradual reductions were made until 1979, when it was decided that the Special Operations Wing should be disbanded, along with other special-forces groups within the United States Armed Forces. As the unit was being prepared for transfer to the reserve status, the incident that has become known as the Iranian Hostage Crisis took place.

This one event temporarily halted the deactivation, and the subsequent diastrous attempt to rescue the hostages finally stopped the relegation. Our government, and some of our senior military leaders, embarrassed at our apparent impotence concerning the Iranian situation, realized that the Air Force Special Operations Wing and other special-forces groups within the U.S. defense structure were a vital and necessary part of any modern military organization.

In 1983, aircraft of the Special Operations Wing were some of the first to see action over the tiny island of Grenada, when they flew support operations for three other elite fighting forces—the Rangers, the Marines, and the SEALs. The combined operations effort of the four groups restored the faith of our public, military, and political leaders, as well as our allies, in our nation's ability to take positive and assertive military action to protect the cause of freedom.

Fortunately, the lessons learned in World War Two and the Vietnam War have not been forgotten. Today, the 1st Special Operations Wing of the 2nd Air Command, based at Hurlburt Field, Florida, is fully operational. It is involved in extensive training and operational programs that will permit it to hone the skills necessary to serve the nation when called to do so.

3
BATTLEFIELD LOG:
Broadway, Burma—March 5, 1944

Throughout Saturday, March 4, and Sunday, March 5, 1944, the P-51A fighters and B-25 bombers of the 1st Air Commando ranged like mad eagles over the north-central area of Burma. Their orders were to fly deep into Burma from their adjoining bases of Lalaghat and Hailakandi in northern India, and to create as much mischief, havoc, and destruction as possible with anything that was Japanese. The orders were eagerly and enthusiastically complied with by the pilots of the Air Commando.

By 1700 hours on Sunday the fighters and bombers had flown over three hundred sorties against the enemy in a so-called softening up operation. They had attacked airfields and aircraft, trains, supply dumps, bridges, boats on the Chindwin and Irrawaddy rivers, columns of troops, radio and radar stations, weather stations, and all manner of enemy vehicles and fortifications. The sorties covered such a large area, appeared to be indiscriminate, and were so diverse in nature that even the pilots and senior officers involved in the operation could not guess which area was going to get the "big stick" that inevitably followed every softening-up operation.

Japanese intelligence documents captured toward the end of the war revealed that their intelligence officers were just as confused by the widespread attacks as were the Air Commando pilots who conducted them. However, before the sun had risen on the morning of March 6, an accidental "disaster" was to further confuse the enemy intelligence organization and greatly assist the Allied commanders in achieving their objective.

At this point in the China/India/Burma war, the Japanese 18th Division was containing the combined American and Chinese armies of General "Vinegar Joe" Stilwell in northern Burma. The British Army, under General William Slim, was also being hard pressed to hold the Japanese along the border between India and Burma.

General Slim was one of a handful of top military men in the Allied forces who knew that almost all the Japanese signal codes had been broken; as a result, he had knowledge that the enemy was reinforcing their army on the central India-Burma border in preparation for the invasion of India. Slim even knew the date of the invasion—March 16, 1944—and he also knew that even if the combined Allied forces in India were placed in front of the advancing enemy, they could not stop the advance.

Although it was a common belief that the British were going to attempt to retake Burma, it was not true. Prime Minister Churchill had informed his own top generals, including Slim, and President Roosevelt that he would not mount an invasion of Burma. It was his belief that the massive American effort in the Pacific would ultimately force the Japanese to withdraw, and all that was required of the present India-Burma campaign was to stop the Japanese from taking India. Roosevelt agreed with Churchill.

With that knowledge, and the knowledge that the Japanese were about to attempt an invasion of India, Slim instigated "Operation Thursday," the code name for a plan of attack that came straight off a chess board.

It was a classic knight's move—a leap over the opposing force's front line with a landing in the middle of enemy-held territory.

The Chindits, in two groups, were to move into the north-central area of Burma between the Irrawaddy River and the Myitkyina–Mandalay railway line. Brigadier Fergusson's 16th Brigade, consisting of some three thousand Chindits, would move around the enemy flank in northern India and march over three hundred miles to get to the area. Approximately four weeks after Fergusson's "foot sloggers" had departed, a further nine thousand Chindits and about fifteen hundred pack mules, the combined forces of Brigadier "Mad Mike" Calvert's 77th Brigade, and Brigadier Joseph Lentaigne's 111th Brigade were to be flown in by the Air Commando.

The purpose of Operation Thursday was to affect the Japanese in the following ways: to cut the supply lines to the Japanese 18th Division, which was stopping the advance of General Stilwell's forces in the north; to force them to remove troops from the Chinese border in the east of Burma, in order to reinforce the center, thereby giving the Chinese Army an opportunity to enter Burma from the east; and, finally, to make the Japanese generals think again about invading India when a large Allied force was attacking their rear.

It was to be a pure commando raid—the Chindits were being sent in for the sole purpose of harassing the enemy; there was no intention, or even a possibility, of the Chindits' driving the Japanese out of Burma. It was, and still is to this day, the largest commando raid ever conducted that far behind enemy lines.

The 1st Air Commando would be "the hand that moved the knight," but that was only their first responsibility. Operation Thursday was not just a quick raid—the Chindits were going to stay for as long as possible, hopefully months—and the Air Commando was to be responsible for providing air cover against enemy planes, air support against the enemy ground forces, and food, drinking water, ammunition, and medical supplies throughout the entire operation, but perhaps the most important job of all would be the evacuation of the sick and wounded. This was important because the morale of the Chindits depended on it, and the commanding generals knew that in the weeks and months to come, morale would be the most significant factor influencing the Chindits' will to fight.

The jungle fighters knew that with Air Commando support they would not be left in the jungle to die from wounds, dysentery, malaria, or some other nefarious tropical disease; and that they would not, because of illness or injury, be left to be taken prisoner by the sadistic and vengeful Japanese—a fate the British soldiers considered worse than death.

During training exercises in the rugged, roadless terrain of northern India, the Chindits had become firmly attached and fiercely loyal to their private American Air Force as a result of one little incident.

All the Chindit groups had Air Commando liaison officers attached. These men were actually pilots who were assigned to the ground forces to coordinate the air support. Philip Cochran believed that the Air Commando could do a better job from the air if they fully understood the problems on the ground, and he ordered a rotation of his pilots to the duty. At first the pilots complained bitterly as the Chindits seemed to frown upon or ignore the flashy American "Brylcreem Boys." (Brylcreem was a hair preparation supposedly used by all members of the British Royal Air Force, hence the nickname used by British soldiers to denote *all* Air Force personnel).

During one particular combined exercise, a British soldier was savagely kicked in the genitals by one of the pack mules, and even the medical orderlies who rushed to assist him were horrified at the damage. The Air Commando liaison officer immediately called for an aircraft to lift the injured man out, much to the surprise of the soldiers surrounding the injured man. Looking around, they saw no clear area where an aircraft could possibly land, and, in disbelief, they asked the Air Commando, "Where?"

The Air Commando simply pointed to a rough open area just behind them and marched off to examine it. The Chindits stared blankly at one another, shook their heads, and then set out after their Brylcreem Boy. The Air Commando quickly paced the area, nodded in satisfaction, and requested that a few large stones and tree trunks be moved to one side. After five minutes he signaled that the area was sufficiently clear, but the soldiers still did not believe him and continued to clear much smaller objects.

Shortly afterward, a small Stinson L-5 came in low over the trees; to the amazement of the Chindits, the pilot did not even hesitate. He made one turn, headed straight for the tiny clearing, and brought his craft to a halt in half the available space. Within minutes, the medics had placed the injured man in the aircraft, and the grinning pilot taxied to the end of the clearing, held the brakes on, ran his engine up to full power, then quickly released the brakes. The watching Chindits held their breath as the L-5 slowly accelerated and bounced along the rough clearing. Just when it seemed that the tiny craft was doomed to collide with the trees at the other end of the clearing, it suddenly leaped into the air, missing the trees by a wide margin.

The jubilant Chindits cheered wildly and almost made a casualty of the Air Commando officer with their grateful but hearty back-slapping gestures.

Word spread fast among the Chindit brigades. Within a matter of hours, morale had soared to unexpected levels as the soldiers realized that rescue from the jungles was possible with the aid of their private air force. The Air Commandos had earned the trust of the fierce and somewhat stoic Chindits.

It was with this continuing spirit of trust and friendship that the Chindit officers and soldiers worked with the Air Commandos as they prepared for the forthcoming operation.

Three reasonably flat, open areas in the middle of the jungle were chosen as the landing areas. They were code-named "Broadway," "Piccadilly," and "Chowringhee."

The first part of the operation called for the Air Commando to land eighty CG-4 gliders, filled with a small, battle-seasoned Chindit fighting force and American airfield engineers and their equipment, at Broadway and Piccadilly; Chowringhee was to be taken three days later.

The plan called for the Chindits to form a defensive perimeter around the areas while the engineers constructed, within twenty-four hours at the most, runways that would permit the remainder of the Chindits to be flown in by a fleet of C-47s.

General Wingate had conceived and engineered the plan, but, despite his brilliance, courage, and leadership abilities, he sometimes made some peculiar and bad decisions. One of these was the strict instruction that exactly one week before the planned assault, all reconnaissance flights over the landing areas would cease. This was not taken kindly by the Air Commando pilots, since all the glider landings were going to be made at night. They protested, but Wingate insisted: *no* reconnaissance flights!

Although General Slim could have ordered Wingate to allow the flights, he did not. Instead, he implied to Phil Cochran that perhaps the Air Commandos' fears could be put to rest by other means. Nothing further was said, and the Air Commando pilots quietly arranged for a B-25 to "accidentally" fly over and photograph all three landing sites just hours before the first wave of gliders was due to be lifted off. If the areas were still clear, nothing would be said; if the areas were not clear, the pilots would inform General Slim.

In the early afternoon of March 5, several B-25s and P-51s took off from Lalaghat airfield on routine missions into northern Burma. However, when they were well clear of Lalaghat, one B-25 suddenly turned east and headed for the north-central area. The unauthorized reconnaissance was under way.

Meanwhile, back at Lalaghat and Hailakandi, some six hundred Chindits and American airfield engineers were preparing to board eighty CG-4A gliders.

The glider pilots were supervising the loading of their craft with the engineers' construction equipment, and great care had to be taken not to damage or overload the frail craft. Four of the glider pilots were horrified as they watched the engineers happily load a wicked-looking bulldozer into each of their craft. The pilots howled their protests about the bulldozers being over-weight, but there was no way out of it—the bulldozers had to be transported in the first wave. The pilots promptly demanded more restraining ropes and straps; they were horrified at the thought of a bulldozer coming loose during the turbulence over the mountains or during a hard landing at night on a rough jungle clearing. One happy-faced engineer, on seeing the number of extra ropes that one pilot and copilot had attached to their bulldozer cargo, suggested that if they had problems getting off the ground they ought to throw away some of the ropes, since they weighed more than the bulldozer. He left quickly when the pilots started after him.

Several other glider pilots offered to change places with those assigned to carry the bulldozers, and at first it seemed like a generous offer. But when it was discovered that the "gracious" pilots had been assigned to carry the Chindits' unpredictable and mean-looking pack mules, those assigned to the bulldozers decided that their cargoes were perhaps not as bad as they had first thought.

Gliders were moved around and arranged in their takeoff order; tow cables with their attached telephone lines were carefully checked and laid out in long rows in preparation for their connection to both gliders and tow planes. To a casual onlooker, the airfield would appear to be a shambles of men, mules, C-47s, gliders, construction equipment, and supplies. To a certain extent, it was, but the ground crews organizing the preparations had everything planned and appeared to know exactly where everything was. The fact that the airfield looked like a shambles did not bother them—everything was organized, and woe betide anyone who tried to change things.

The B-25 pilot had studied the positions of the proposed landing sites and had plotted a course that was a straight line, running from north to south, almost directly over all three areas. Broadway was the northernmost landing site, Piccadilly was some thirty miles south of it, and Chowringhee was almost eighty miles south of Piccadilly. By flying his aircraft in a continuous line, there was much less chance of the enemy guessing that it was a preinvasion reconnaissance mission. The pilot knew that he could not risk circling over the areas and could not make a second pass—he had to get the photographs on the first run.

From the air it was clear to see that Broadway and Chowringhee were just as they had been a week earlier, but Piccadilly was drastically changed. The pilot caught his breath as he saw the landing area covered with neat rows of huge teak logs—it would be impossible for a glider to land there in daylight, let alone under cover of darkness. Worried about the possibility of a camera failure, the pilot considered making another run, but his navigator/cameraman assured him that he had used two cameras and that he had taken enough photographs on the first pass. It was almost 1600 hours, and the first wave of gliders was to take off at 1800 hours. There was very little time left for them to get safely back to Lalaghat and warn Cochran.

Despite the fact that the B-25 was flying at maximum speed, the journey seemed to take forever. Time was running out, and when they finally landed at Lalaghat, the pilot alarmed the ground crews by ignoring their marshaling signals and taxiing right across the airfield to the photography tent. Within minutes the film was developed and printed, and the photography officer and the B-25 pilot raced outside and commandeered a Jeep.

They raced to nearby Hailakandi airfield at breakneck speed; on arriving there, they spotted the distinct figure of General Slim talking to Wingate, Calvert, Cochran, and several other high-ranking officers. It was 1745 hours when the Jeep, with a screech of breaks in a small cloud of dust, pulled up beside General Slim. The two reconnaissance men were somewhat nervous as they handed Slim the still-wet photograph, and they managed just one word: "Piccadilly."

When Wingate saw the photograph he was furious. But it was not clear whether he was annoyed because his orders had been disobeyed by the Air Commando pilots or because he thought the operation had been blown. In any event, Wingate wanted the entire operation scrubbed—he was convinced that information had been leaked to the enemy by the Chinese and that the situation had been further compromised by the unauthorized reconnaissance flight.

Slim knew that the Chinese had nothing to do with it because they had never been informed of the exact nature of the operation, nor did he believe that there had been any compromise with the photo-reconnaissance mission. He and almost everyone else knew that certain disaster had been avoided by the Air Commando's foresight and somewhat impudent action. He asked the reconnaissance pilot about Broadway and Chowringhee, and when he learned that both landing areas were still clear, he ordered that the operation proceed—with a few changes.

Piccadilly was scrubbed, and instead of eighty gliders being sent only sixty were to go—all of them to Broadway. Chowringhee would be assaulted, as planned, three days later.

Some rapid rearranging of men, mules, and equipment took place, and the number of gliders was increased to sixty-one. With the rearranging completed, Colonel Cochran briefed the pilots. Although he wanted to participate in the raid, he had been persuaded by General Slim and several of his own men that he should remain in India and coordinate operations from Slim's headquarters.

Despite the last-minute panic and rearranging, the first C-47 trundled down the runway at 1812 hours—with *two* fully laden gliders in tow—and the airborne stage of Operation Thursday was under way.

The decision to have one C-47 towing two gliders was a controversial one. There was no doubt that the C-47 was capable of it under normal circumstances, but this mission required that the gliders be loaded to their maximum capacity, and, in that condition, they would have to be towed to a height of at least eighty-five hundred feet to clear the Naga Mountains.

Major Thomas Baker, the commanding officer of the transport group (and the man who devised the first emblem of the Air Commando), was completely against a two-glider tow. He felt that the drag of two fully laden gliders, which he knew would be loaded far in excess of their rated maximum capacity, would cause severe overheating problems on the C-47 engines during the climb in the thin mountain air. Apart from the inherent dangers of overheating, the fuel consumption of the aircraft would be both incredibly high and unpredictable, and he was certain that some aircraft would finish the climb only to find that they did not have sufficient fuel to get to the landing area, drop the pickles, and return to Hailakandi.

Baker also knew that when they hit the mountain turbulence, which there was no way of avoiding, the glider pilots would be so intent on trying to keep their craft upright and away from each other that they could either tear off the tail of the tow ship or create so much drag that the C-47s would be stalled in midair.

Another of his concerns was that he only had thirteen C-47s and it was going to take thirty-one of them to tow sixty-one gliders. Air Transport Command was to provide the extra C-47s, and, since Baker had no spare personnel, they would also provide the crews. Despite his respect for the high level of flying skill of the Transport Command pilots, Baker knew that most of them had absolutely no experience at towing a glider, let alone two that were fully laden!

Baker was not scare-mongering—-he and his group of Air Commando transport pilots were perhaps the most experienced C-47/CG-4 tow pilots in the world. They had all performed two-glider tows and some had even towed three of the lumbering craft in an unladen condition. Major Baker's concern was based on solid experience, and he warned Cochran that he should expect to lose as many as half of the total glider force—long before they reached the landing area.

However, Baker and his men lost the battle. Phil Cochran felt it was worth the risk and decided to proceed with the two-glider tow.

The leading elements of "Mad Mike" Calvert's 77th Brigade and the airfield engineers were now firmly strapped in the gliders awaiting their turn for takeoff. As the first C-47 lifted off the ground with its pair of pickles in tow, the second C-47 lined up with the runway and took up the slack of the tow ropes. Moments later it started down the runway as the sun dipped down behind the trees surrounding the airfield.

The third pair of gliders was pulled on the runway and the tow ropes and telephone lines were connected. The glider on the right-hand side of the C-47 was piloted by the deputy commander of the Air Commando, Colonel John Alison, who had quickly learned to fly the gliders just a few days before the operation began. Alison was a fighter pilot who had been flying P-40 fighters with the famous Flying Tigers before General Arnold assigned him, along with Phil Cochran, the job of cocommander of the 1st Air Commando. Alison was in the spearhead wave of gliders because his job on Broadway was perhaps one of the more vital.

The first glider to land in the clearing was flown by one of the most experienced of the Air Commando glider pilots. He was effectively the *pathfinder* because, apart from a supposedly unobstructed clearing in the jungle, there was nothing to guide him. When, and if, his glider landed safely, he would light small kerosene "smudge pots" to indicate his position on the ground. This would ensure that the next few gliders, including Alison's, would not land on top of him; and when Alison was safely on the ground, he would organize a string of temporary runway lights to guide the remainder of the CG-4As to a safe landing.

When all the gliders were down, Alison was to organize the building of the airstrip for the powered craft, and he had to complete that job within twelve hours of the last glider's landing. Once the runway was constructed, he was to act as "airport" manager and air-traffic controller to organize and coordinate the incoming waves of C-47s, which would be filled with the remainder of Calvert's brigade.

The first C-47 off the runway at Hailakandi took forty-five minutes to climb eighty-five hundred feet. It was something of a nightmare for the pilot as he watched his engine and oil temperature gauges move rapidly up past the recommended limits, while his fuel gauge was moving equally fast in the opposite direction. There were long moments when his aircraft was barely climbing as the two heavily laden gliders snatched and tugged at the C-47's tail. It was almost as if they were deliberately trying to drag the tow ship to its doom, and the C-47 pilot swore at them for the full forty-five minutes it took to reach eighty-five hundred feet.

For the glider pilots, the worst part was the takeoff—

they had to fight to keep their cumbersome craft away from each other when they had barely enough speed to control them. However, once they were airborne and had effective control of their machines, they easily settled into the long, steady, circling climb.

With its nose high in the air, its fuel being burned away at an alarming rate, its engines hotter than they had ever been, and its pilot threatening to cut the pickles off if he saw one more degree increase in the engine or oil temperature, the overloaded and overworked C-47 reached eighty-five hundred feet.

As the sweating pilot allowed the nose of his aircraft to drop to cruise attitude, he eased back on the throttles. The fuel consumption immediately dropped to an acceptable level. The engine and oil temperatures did not drop, however, and it would be almost a half-hour before the pilot saw sufficient drop to allow himself to relax. He checked the figures that his copilot gave him on the fuel status—they had enough for the mission, but there was no margin for error.

The turbulence came as expected, and with it came the usual violent ride—but it was much worse towing two gliders. The C-47 pilot used all his skill, and every expletive he knew, as he fought the turbulence and the rampaging gliders that appeared determined to tear his aircraft apart or crash into each other.

When the turbulence finally stopped, life on board the powered craft and the gliders became somewhat more bearable, not only for the pilots but for the fully armed Chindits—fifteen crowded into each CG-4A. Most of the Chindits had never been in an aircraft before—glider or powered—and they had no desire to get in one again after their experience in the turbulence over the Patkai and Naga mountains.

The C-47 pilot concentrated his attention on navigating an accurate course to Broadway and periodically called his position back to the glider pilots. The glider pilots lightly marked their maps with pencil each time they received the position report; it coincided with their own navigation, and that knowledge helped them to relax a little. Knowing exactly where they were, in the event of a tow rope breaking or an emergency cutaway, was a vital aid to the glider crews when it came to a forced landing and their chances of survival behind enemy lines.

As the men in the lead C-47 settled down for the remaining two hours of flight to Broadway, Major Tom Baker's concerns about the two-glider tow were being justified.

Shortly after takeoff, every C-47 pilot realized that two fully laden gliders stretched the valiant Gooney Birds beyond their maximum rated ability. On the climb to altitude, some engines overheated to the point of seizing, and tow-ship pilots cut their pickles free to fend for themselves. Some aircraft managed to get to eighty-five hundred feet only to find that their engines would not cool down sufficiently to permit their journey to continue and they were compelled to turn back. Some, with similar engine problems, managed to get east to the Chindwin River before their overstressed engines finally either refused to continue with the load of two gliders or refused to function at all. As a result, the hapless gliders were cut loose deep in enemy territory, while the C-47s struggled back to India or crashed in the jungle when the engines finally gave out.

Some of the tow groups were subjected to such severe turbulence that several tow ropes frayed and parted, leaving unfortunate glider pilots to fend for themselves.

Other C-47 pilots found that their craft had consumed so much fuel during the climb to altitude that they had insufficient reserves to complete the journey and were forced to return to the airfield.

Of the sixty-one gliders that left India, problems with the tow ships and breaking ropes were the cause of eight landing in friendly territory and a further ten landing over a wide area behind enemy lines east of the

Chindwin River. Of the ten that landed behind enemy lines, eight were actually accounted for; the other two gliders simply disappeared and were never found.

As the lead C-47 approached Broadway, the glider pilots were called and informed that the approach was being made from the south and east, as all indications were that the winds were still out of the northwest. The glider pilots had requested that, if possible, they be released at one thousand feet directly over the jungle clearing, with their noses pointing into the wind. From that point they would make one sweeping 360-degree turn and attempt to land into the wind on the faintly moonlit clearing.

The glider pilots informed the Chindits that they were on the run in the landing area. There was a flurry of activity, and the metallic sounds of magazines being slapped into weapons, rounds being rammed into empty breeches, and the harsh clack of automatic pistols being cocked and readied. Despite the noise created by the rushing air over the exteriors of the craft, the glider pilots heard all those foreign noises and were somewhat startled by them. The sounds stopped almost as quickly as they had started, and the pilots knew that the fierce-looking Chindits were ready to go about their deadly business. All that was required now was to get them safely on the ground.

Nervous, last-minute thoughts flooded through the glider pilots' minds as they approached Broadway. They realized that they were virtually landing blind and that the soldiers sitting behind them trusted their flying skills with an almost equal blindness. The pilots knew that there was no way of knowing if the clearing was really suitable; there could be hidden logs, tree stumps, and deep ruts in the long grass. And there was the possibility that the whole area was mined or surrounded by a large enemy force. When the clearing came in sight, such thoughts were pushed from their minds. As they flew directly over the strip, the lead glider pilot released his tow line, and the second glider pilot followed his action moments later.

The C-47 pilot felt his aircraft respond instantly with a slight shudder and a steady forward surge. It was almost as if the aircraft were a living creature responding to the removal of a tremendous burden; and as the pilot pulled the craft away toward the west he had a feeling of tremendous relief as the aircraft responded to his control inputs in a manner that he had almost forgotten during the grueling tow. When he was well clear of Broadway, he released his trailing tow ropes, and, as they fell into the jungle below, the C-47 responded again with a tiny increase in speed.

The lead glider pilot had a good look at the open area beneath him as he made his descending turn. Mentally, he chose a "runway" in the middle of the clearing and committed himself to landing on it. As he approached the end of the clearing he eased the nose forward to maintain his speed of one hundred miles per hour. He quickly and carefully made an assessment of his height as the craft neared the ground—perhaps the most diffi-cult thing to do in landing any aircraft on a darkened strip—and then gently pulled up the nose as the craft started to sink.

The sudden slapping of tall grass along the bottom of the fuselage was the first telltale sound that signified he had judged the sink rate correctly. It was a sound he had been hoping and waiting for, but it surprised and scared the tense Chindits behind him. As the grass slapped the fuselage, the pilot started to pull steadily back on the control yoke to hold the glider off the ground until it ran out of flying speed. This was a critical movement—if he pulled the yoke back too quickly, the craft could balloon upward and lose flying speed far too rapidly. The result would be the craft's stalling some twenty or thirty feet in the air and then dropping violently to the ground in a landing that could only be called a crash because of the inevitable damage.

Just as the pilot had the yoke back as far as it would

go, the massive glider settled on firm ground in a perfect touchdown. There was a great shuddering and grinding noise as the machine then bumped and bounced along the rough clearing. The noise became a little less frightening to the Chindits strapped inside the darkened glider as it started to slow down. Suddenly, the craft swung to the right and jerked to a halt, but its energy was spent and no damage was done.

For a long moment there was silence. The sudden sound of seatbelts being released and the glider nose being unlatched broke the silence. Chindits raced past the pilots into the clearing and immediately fanned out into a defensive ring around the craft. The second glider landed a short distance away, swung wickedly to one side, and came to a halt with a violent crunching sound as one of its wheels was torn off by a hidden log. Apart from a few bruises, no one was hurt, and within seconds Chindits were scrambling out and taking up their positions.

The kerosene smudges were lit as the deep droning sound of another C-47 was heard. As a small scouting patrol of Chindits raced off into the dense jungle, the aircraft and its two gliders came into view in the pale moonlit sky.

The gliders slipped the tow lines, and as they swept in a tight circle and approached the clearing, they made a strange sighing noise. The pilots of the two gliders already on the ground watched as the next pair of gliders approached, barely missing the trees at the edge of the clearing. The first one landed safely and soldiers rushed out of it, but the second one hit an obstruction and the landing wheels were torn off. The craft slid a short distance and looked as if it was about to turn tail over nose, but somehow it remained sound amid a cloud of dust. As men raced toward it, Chindits were seen scrambling out of the craft; again, there were no serious injuries.

The next pair of gliders had been cut loose overhead; one of them was being flown by John Alison, and the other was carrying Brigadier Calvert and half his head-quarters' staff. Alison landed his craft without incident, but Calvert's glider hit a rut just before it came to a halt and the landing wheels were torn away. There were no injuries on board, and Calvert and the men in the aircraft came charging out as if it were a perfect landing.

Alison took a quick look around and realized that the gliders already on the strip were about to become a hazard. He organized some men to try to move the wrecks just as the next pair of engineless craft came rushing down. The lead machine of this pair turned too low over the edge of the jungle, and one of its wings caught in the treetops. There was a violent tearing and crashing sound as the glider disappeared below the trees. When the noise of the crash settled down, wounded men could be heard screaming in agony. Medics and a doctor fought their way through the brush to get to them.

The second glider managed to clear the trees and flared out close to the ground; just as it touched the ground it found a hidden obstruction, lurched violently around, and slid backward along the ground with one of its wings broken and twisted. It came to a halt resting on its good wing but facing in the direction from which it had just come.

By now, John Alison had discovered that the glider carrying the temporary runway lights and "airport" control equipment was missing, so he quickly set about improvising a lighting system. As he started to exchange the existing smudge lights, another pair of gliders came down into the confusion. One of the pilots managed to use the last of his flying speed to lift his craft over a wrecked glider, and he landed roughly, but safely, beyond it. The pilot of the second glider obviously did not see the wreck—he flew straight into it at about ninety miles per hour. When the terrible crashing noise stopped, the nightmarish screams of the wounded filled the clearing. Again, medics raced to help, but most of the men were to lose their lives.

Alison managed to move the lights clear of the wrecks before the next wave of gliders dropped from behind their tired tow ships. Most of this wave landed safely enough, inasmuch as the gliders were wrecked but there were few injuries. The next wave was not so lucky—two gliders hit the treetops and crashed badly in the clearing, killing a few more men and wounding several others.

Calvert's first patrols were returning from the jungle to report that there was no sign of the Japanese. Apart from the minimum number of men required to defend the clearing, Calvert assigned everyone to Alison and his crew of engineers to help move the wrecked gliders that were now threatening to ruin the operation.

The next wave of gliders carried the first bulldozer, and the pilot made a perfect approach, only to find his chosen landing area blocked by a wrecked glider. He skillfully avoided hitting it, then was horrified to see another set of wreckage just in front of him. He kicked the rudder pedal hard to avoid the wreckage and plowed straight into the jungle between two trees. As the glider entered the jungle at about sixty miles per hour, its wings were ripped off by the tree trunks. The fuselage came to a violent stop in the undergrowth, but the force of the impact and the sudden stop broke the restraining straps on the bulldozer, and it shot forward into the cockpit, blade first. The helpless pilot and copilot were hurled upward, and the charging monster shot out the front of the glider into the jungle and came to a halt some thirty feet away. The pilots landed on the ground behind the bulldozer, which had not been damaged during its rapid exit from the glider. The men were bruised but otherwise unhurt, and as they sat on the jungle floor staring at each other, the pilot laconically informed his copilot that he had planned to unload it that way.

With the first bulldozer down, wrecked gliders were more easily moved to keep the landing area clear, and by 0400 hours a total of thirty-five gliders had landed on Broadway; apart from three craft, none of the others would fly again. It was at this point that Calvert and Alison decided to call a halt to the glider operation.

The moon had now gone down, and despite the lights on the clearing they felt that further landings would simply incur more disasters and cause more deaths and injuries. The casualty figure stood at thirty dead and thirty-three wounded. Calvert and Alison felt that they had enough Chindits for defense, enough construction equipment, and sufficient engineers to operate it to get the runway built within the next twelve to fourteen hours.

A signal was sent to Cochran and Slim to turn back the remaining gliders.

When dawn broke, the American engineers and every available Chindit set to work on building the runway. They had no sooner started than the sound of aircraft engines made them look up; they saw a neat formation of Air Commando L-5 liaison/ambulance planes sweep over the treetops. The pilots had attached long-range tanks to their tiny unarmed craft and had flown from India through the dangerous mountain passes and then at treetop level over the jungle to reach Broadway. As soon as they landed, the pilots talked to Alison, then several of them took off immediately to search the nearby jungle for missing gliders.

Before darkness fell that evening, a runway some five thousand feet long and three hundred feet wide—complete with improvised landing lights—had been constructed, and the Chindits had dug a series of good defensive positions around the perimeter.

John Alison had turned a wrecked glider into a control tower, and as darkness fell he guided the first C-47 into Broadway. Shortly afterward, it took off again with all the wounded men on board.

By dawn the next morning, sixty-two C-47s of both Air Commando and Air Transport Command had landed, disembarked fully armed Chindits and supplies, and had taken off again for further men and supplies. Within the next five days, some nine thousand Chindits, twelve hundred mules, and three hundred tons of equipment and supplies were flown by C-47s into the heart of Japanese-held Burma.

The Japanese were slow to react, due primarily to the fact that they had been totally confused by the unfortunate gliders that had been forced to land over an area of over a hundred square miles throughout north-central Burma. The aircraft that had crashed—both C-47s and CG-4s—had not gone down in vain. They had inadvertently acted as decoys, by misleading the Japanese and ensuring the success of Operation Thursday on the makeshift runway of Broadway.

4

AIRCRAFT OF THE AIR COMMANDO DURING WORLD WAR TWO

It is interesting to note that the old Air Commando and the presentday Special Operations Wing have never had an aircraft designed and built especially for their own use. They have always taken aircraft from the existing Air Force inventory and modified them to meet their own specific requirements.

This practice continues, and it is reasonably safe to say that, out of necessity, almost all aircraft in today's Special Operations Wing are hybrid. However, such aircraft were not castoffs from other units; they were chosen for modification because of their proven performance in other areas of operation.

C-47
Perhaps the most used and the most famous of the Air Commando and Special Operations Wing aircraft is the venerable twin-engined C-47 (the C designates "Transport"). The C-47 is also the aircraft that has been given more names, or type designations, than any other aircraft in aviation history. It was otherwise known by its

civilian name, the DC-3; its U.S. Navy name, the R4D; its old Army Air Force names, the C-47A, C-47B, AC-47 (A stands for Attack, Armed, or Advanced, depending on the type of aircraft it is applied to); TC-47B (T stands for Training), SC-47 (S stands for Scout, and this variant was used for air/sea rescue); C-48, C-49, C-50, C-51, C-52, C-53, C-68, C-84, and C-117. The British called it the Dakota, and it was also known by nicknames such as the Gooney Bird, Spooky, the Dragonship, and the Skytrain.

Regardless of the designations applied to this remarkable aircraft (usually because of some minor change in operational mode, engine type, interior cabin arrangement, or if an aircraft was impressed from civil airlines for military use), it was always recognizable as a C-47/ DC-3. It was in limited service, in one form or another, with the Army Air Force from about 1936 to 1940 and was first ordered as the C-47 in large quantities in 1940.

It normally had a crew of three: pilot, copilot, and one other—either a radio operator, navigator, engineer, or cargomaster, depending on the theater or mode of operation. It had a maximum speed of 230 miles per hour and a range of about fifteen hundred miles. It could carry between twenty-six and thirty fully armed combat troops, or about eight thousand pounds of cargo. A total of about thirteen thousand aircraft were built, some two thousand of which were built under license in the Soviet Union and about five hundred in Japan.

The C-47/DC-3 was the aerial workhorse of the Allied forces in every theater of World War Two, and at the end of the war, General Dwight D. Eisenhower said that it was one of four major tools that had contributed to the Allied victory.

The first Air Commando C-47s that arrived in India were actually civilian DC-3s that had been impressed from several American airline companies. They were somewhat more luxurious than the traditional military

C-47s, much to the delight of the 1st Air Commando pilots who flew them.

All the C-47s were unarmed. For protection, the pilots relied on darkness during night operations and their own fighter aircraft during daylight operations. Apart from general transportation duties, such as troop carrying, mule carrying, medical evacuation, and normal and air-dropped cargo supply operations, the Air Commando C-47 aircraft and their pilots were perhaps most famous for their exploits involving gliders.

As well as towing the fully laden craft off the ground, the Air Commando pilots perfected the technique of retrieving the gliders from the ground as they flew their C-47s over them at a speed of 120 miles per hour. Contrary to what might be believed, the actual pickup, from both the C-47 and the glider pilots, points of view, was quite a gentle affair, assuming it was done correctly using the proper equipment. The gentle pickup, as explained in chapter 1, was due to the use of a nylon tow rope that was attached to the glider and the use of an automatic winch in the C-47.

The C-47/DC-3 is still in use in large numbers throughout the world. In the United States it is used mostly for cargo carrying, heavy multiengine pilot training, and executive transportation, and at least one major commuter airline is still using it to carry passengers. In other regions of the world, particularly in remote areas, this rugged and reliable craft is used extensively for both cargo and passenger transportation, and it is still used by the armed forces of various third-world and emerging nations.

From a pilot's point of view, the C-47 is a pleasure to fly. Like a good car, it handles well, it is stable, and, although it is a little slow, it is responsive to control inputs. It is not without its quirks or little vices, but those are really quite minor, and in the hands of any reasonably experienced pilot it is a safe and trustworthy craft. Finally, it is easy to maintain and repair, and it will take a considerable amount of punishment from the rough handling of inexperienced pilots, as well as poor or neglected runways and landing strips.

UC-64

The *UC* designated Light Transport, and the UC-64 was clearly in this category. Called the Norseman, it was a large, single-engined, high-winged, six- to eight-passenger aircraft of Canadian manufacture, and it was built specifically as a "bush plane" for the remote Canadian territories. The Army Air Force purchased a small number of the craft because of its ability to carry heavy loads in and out of short and rough landing strips; Phil Cochran chose it for the Air Commando for the same reason.

It was an extremely reliable and rugged aircraft, and most people were not aware of its use by the Army Air Force until one carrying the famous bandleader Glenn Miller disappeared somewhere between England and France. No trace of the unarmed Norseman or its occupants was ever found, and it was presumed that it was either shot down or suffered a mechanical failure and crashed into the sea.

The Air Commando found that the UC-64 was ideally suited to their needs, particularly as it could be used to tow the TG training gliders and unloaded CG-4s on practice flights. However, it was better suited to air-dropping supplies to the Chindits in the jungle, and it also served as an ambulance aircraft.

Only a handful of Air Commando pilots flew the craft, perhaps because there were so few of them available, but those who flew it claimed it was an easy aircraft to fly and presented no major problems during operation.

The Norseman is still in use today, in the Canadian wilderness, in the role it was originally designed for—that of a bush plane.

CG-4

The CG-4 glider was designed by the Waco Company of Troy, Ohio, and almost fourteen thousand of the engineless craft were built by a conglomerate of sixteen companies during World War Two. The boxlike fuselage was constructed of tubular steel and covered with fabric and thin plywood. The large wings were built with thin ribs attached to a wooden main spar, and they too were covered with fabric and thin plywood.

The CG-4 was fitted with elementary controls and flight instruments and normally carried a crew of two: pilot and copilot. Two side doors were installed, one under each wing, to permit access for the pilots and the loading of troops. Although troop-carrying capacity was limited to thirteen fully armed men, the small size of the glider made it ideal for towing either with large single-engined, or with small twin-engined, aircraft such as the C-47.

In the event that cargo—such as a Jeep, bulldozer, small artillery piece, pack mules, or other bulky objects— had to be carried, the complete nose, or cockpit section, would open upward on hinges to permit easy access to the interior.

No other transport glider was ever built in such large numbers or was more widely used, despite its relatively small load-carrying capacity.

A considerable number were supplied to the British, who named it the Hanibal, in keeping with their practice of identifying gliders with words that began with the letter *H*., e.g., the British-built Horsa and Hamilcar, which could carry twenty-five and fifty men respectfully. These larger gliders, along with their American counterpart, the forty-two–man Waco CG-13, were not as versatile as the CG-4, as they required large four-engined aircraft to tow them when they were fully loaded. Four-engined transport tow planes were not plentiful during World War Two, hence the popularity of the CG-4.

In flight, the CG-4 was fairly easy to handle, provided that the speed was kept up over one hundred miles per hour and that turbulence was avoided. They were designed to land safely in a short distance on rough ground, and during early test flights a famous aerobatic stunt pilot, Mike Murphy, was called upon to crash them into woods, hedgerows, and all manner of obstacles to demonstrate their survivability. The CG-4 apparently passed all these crash-landing tests, and so did Murphy, as he was called upon to give a final demonstration by landing in the middle of a lake. The Army staff had been eager to see if the craft would float long enough to enable men to get out, but the test and design engineers would not commit to the test since they had no idea what would happen. Murphy was finally asked if he would care to do it, and, to most people's amazement, he immediately agreed. On the appointed day, a C-47 flown by Major Thomas Baker, who was to become one of the first Air Commando pilots, towed the CG-4 over the designated lake.

Murphy cut loose from the tow over the middle of the lake and calmly landed the glider, with an impressive splash, in front of a group of generals and other high-ranking officers. A fraction of a second after it had hit the water, the glider suddenly appeared to nose dive for the bottom of the lake. For a few moments it remained with its tail up in the air and the cockpit underwater—like a duck searching for food in a shallow pond—then the tail slowly settled back down and part of the cockpit became visible, much to everyone's relief.

The observers on the lakeside and the crews of the fast-moving rescue boats now watched intently for Murphy to appear from the wreck. As the CG-4 slowly started to sink, they began to get alarmed. There was no sign of life around the slowly sinking glider. The rescue boats were now at the wreck, and the CG-4 was almost totally submerged, but still there was no sign of its pilot. The boat crews had just about given up hope when there was a sudden commotion on the shore of the lake. The generals and other high-ranking officers were jumping up and down and waving frantically toward the water's edge, where a smiling and somewhat bedraggled Murphy was walking out of the water.

He had left the glider moments after it had hit the water, and, as everyone was intently watching the stricken craft, he had been calmly swimming to the shore.

Mike Murphy was also involved in the early trials with the glider-pickup technique. On one occasion, during a test, the C-47 came in a little too fast. Murphy, who was sitting at the controls of the glider waiting to be snatched off the ground, remembered thinking that the C-47 seemed to be moving a little quickly as it passed overhead. However, there was nothing he could do about it except hope that the hook trailing behind the C-47 missed the "clothesline" tow rope. The pilot's aim was good; Murphy saw the hook snag the tow rope and he braced himself. There was a tremendous crash, and when the dust settled, Murphy was sitting on the ground in front of the glider with the control wheel still in his hand. As he looked up, he saw the C-47 pulling away with just the nose of the glider swinging wildly on the end of the tow rope. Mike Murphy continued to work as a test pilot, stunt pilot, and competition aerobatic pilot for many years, both during and after the war. He was one of the founders of the aerobatic-competition movement in the United States and was highly active in the sport of aerobatics between 1950 and 1980.

Almost all the Air Commando pilots who flew the CG-4s were qualified only to fly gliders. Although a considerable number of them had received extensive flight training in powered craft, they had failed their final tests and had applied to fly the gliders just to be flying. There were some pilots, however, who had no previous flying experience in any type of aircraft; they had simply volunteered to fly gliders because it was something different and was an almost certain way to get into action. The Air Commando glider pilots were known by most who came in contact with them as a carefree, gum-chewing bunch, but few envied them their job.

L-1 and L-5

The *L* stands for Liaison, and these aircraft were variants of existing civilian aircraft known as Stinsons. They were tiny aircraft—the L-1 was a two-seater with a radial engine; and the L-5 was similar but had a more modern, horizontally opposed engine (not unlike a Volkswagen engine) and a backseat that could just about hold two people.

They were ordered by the Army Air Force as liaison, reconnaissance, and artillery-spotting aircraft, and they were capable of landing on and taking off from rough air strips, pastures, and jungle clearings of three hundred to four hundred feet long. The L-1 was known as the Vigilant and the L-5 was known as the Sentinel. They had a maximum speed of 130 miles per hour, a range of about 450 miles, and they were completely unarmed.

The Air Commando pilots relied on their skill at low flying and on the maneuverability of their craft to avoid enemy aircraft and ground fire. They became famous in the role of airborne ambulances, and they were perhaps the biggest morale boosters the British Chindits had, because in the hands of the Air Commando pilots they were used primarily to lift disease-ridden and wounded men out of tiny jungle clearings, hilltops, and river sandbars to transport them to field hospitals, or to airfields where they could be transferred to C-47s and taken to hospitals in India.

The L-1 and L-5 aircraft were also used for almost every imaginable military task, from searching for downed pilots, to supplying water, medical supplies, food, replacement radios, and even ammunition in some cases. Modifications by the Air Commando included the fitting of "hard points," or shackles, beneath the wings, from which were suspended two-hundred-pound "bombs" of food and supplies. The tiny L-5s would then struggle

The Air Force's 1st Air Commando Squadron pilots who flew two or more missions through heavy groundfire in front of an **A-1E Skyraider** (1966).

Members of Det-3 of the 1st Air Commando Group in training at Howard Air Force Base, Canal Zone, 1962.

A member of the Combat Control Team.

A UH-1N Huey helicopter.

A U.S. Air Force A-1E Skyraider leaves contrails from its wing tips as it turns to make a bombing pass against a Vietcong concentration in the jungle below.

An Air Force B-57 enroute to bomb a Vietcong storage area in South Vietnam (1966).

An armed A-1, escorting a 40th Aerospace Rescue and Recover Squadron HH-53 helicopter to pick up a downed airman (Vietnam 1972).

Armed with 250-pound general purpose bombs, an A-1E Skyraider taxis for take-off at Pleiku Air Base, South Vietnam (1966).

A mechanic working on the 1st Special Operations Squadron A-1 "Priscilla's Phoenix" in Nanken Phano Air Base, Thailand (1972).

Two 1st Special Operations Squadron, A-1, in fight over the jungles of Southeast Asia, carrying various types of armament (1972).

A B-26 aircraft and pilot participating in the Strike Command exercise Goldfire I in the area of Fort Leonard Wood, Missouri in 1964.

Capt. George W. Grill, Jr., kneels in front of an A-1E Skyraider while on alert duty. During the first five months of 1966, he flew eighty-two missions.

Air Force Lt. Col. Eugene P. Dietrick commands the 1st Air Commando Squadron at Pleiku Air Base in South Vietnam (1966).

A student receives last minute instruction on spray controls from Sgt. James E. Wellerman of the 1st Special Operations Wing (1969).

U.S. Air Force Maj. Bernard F. Fisher, an A-1E
Skyraider pilot, treats Vietnamese children to
American chewing gum (1966).

into the air and seek out the Chindit patrols in the jungle. Flying low and as slow as possible, the pilots would release their "bombs" and literally place them at the feet of the troops.

There were several incidents involving enthusiastic L-5 pilots carrying real fragmentation bombs on the wing shackles of their tiny craft and then acting as bombers to aid groups of beleaguered Chindits, much to the surprise of both the Chindits and the Japanese. It appears that the technique was highly successful on almost every occasion, because of the accuracy of the bombing and because the Japanese immediately withdrew, fearing that a major air assault was in progress.

On numerous occasions, machine-gun-carrying soldiers would unofficially "hitch" a ride with a willing pilot and harass the enemy from the air. Although the effectiveness of this procedure was justifiably questioned, it appears that it did break up several enemy assaults, possibly because of the confusion it caused.

Throughout the war, both in Burma and in the Pacific, the 1st, 2nd, and 3rd Air Commando bush pilots performed some remarkable feats in their L-1s and L-5s, and they were truly some of the most unknown and unsung heroes of the war in the air.

Many of the tiny aircraft, some immaculately restored in their World War Two Commando colors, are still flying today in the hands of civilian sports pilots and aviation enthusiasts. Some of the remarkable little aircraft are actually owned by veterans of the Air Commando who flew them in battle.

P-51 (F-51)

The *P* designates Pursuit, *F* designates Fighter, but regardless of the confusion of the military designators, the P-51 (called the Mustang) has become known as one of the finest fighter aircraft of World War Two. More than fifteen thousand were built, in one form or another, and they were credited with having destroyed almost five thousand enemy aircraft in the air and over four thousand on the ground. Phil Cochran and John Alison managed to persuade General Arnold to let them have thirty of these new fighters for the 1st Air Commando, to the annoyance of almost all the senior Army Air Force commanders, who were desperate to have the new fighters in their own theaters of operation.

The aircraft was originally designed, developed, and manufactured by the North American Aviation Company at the request of the British Royal Air Force, and the first production models were sent to England. The Army Air Force had an arrangement with the British to test and evaluate the aircraft and to acquire it if they so chose. Initial tests showed that a superior aircraft was in the making, and the Army Air Force exercised its option to purchase the fighter, in conjunction with North American and the British government.

The P-51A variant came off the production line in 1943 and had a top speed of 390 miles per hour. It had four machine guns and could carry a thousand pounds of bombs, but the Air Commando mechanics performed various unofficial modifications to permit these craft to carry either extra ammunition or extra bombs. Although it had a range of only 750 miles with its internal tanks, this could easily be extended with the addition of external fuel tanks.

It was a highly maneuverable fighter, relatively easy to fly, and more than a match for the Japanese fighters in Burma. The Air Commando, as was its practice, did not use them solely as fighters. They also used them to supply the Chindits with water, in the form of bombs made from long-range fuel tanks (as described earlier), and as fighter bombers to attack Japanese defensive positions and supply columns. They attacked trains, tanks, and trucks, boats on the Irrawaddy and Chindwin rivers, and almost anything Japanese that moved on the ground or in the air.

They acted as escorts for all other Air Commando aircraft, and whenever the Chindits called for assistance on the ground, the nearest patrolling P-51s were invariably sent to assist in whatever manner they could. After the war, captured enemy intelligence documents indicated that the Japanese believed there were hundreds of the dreaded, diagonal-striped Air Commando fighters operating over Burma. This confusion was caused simply because of Cochran's skillful deployment tactics— the multiple-role use of the P-51s, and constant patrolling, even in the worst weather conditions.

Today there are some P-51s in operation with the air forces of some emerging nations, and there are about one hundred privately owned P-51s still flying in the United States and Europe.

B-25

The B-25 bomber, also called the Mitchell, was named after General William "Billy" Mitchell, who was court-martialed in 1925 for his outspoken criticism of the Chiefs of Staff and their reluctance to develop the nation's air-power capability.

This twin-engined bomber was developed and built by the North American Aviation Company. It had a maximum speed of 315 miles per hour, was heavily armed, and could carry 3,000 pounds of bombs.

It became famous on April 18, 1942, in the hands of Lieutenant Colonel James H. Doolittle and fifteen other pilots when it became the largest aircraft ever to take off from an aircraft carrier. Doolittle, in a hair-raising escapade, led a flight of sixteen fully laden B-25s off the deck of the USS *Hornet* on the first daylight raid on Tokyo. It was a one-way mission, as the aircraft did not have the range to reach the target area and return to a U.S. base. The B-25s were crash-landed in China after their successful raid, which was carried out for psychological rather than practical effect. The plan worked in two ways—it made the Japanese realize that they were vulnerable, and it was a tremendous boost to morale in the United States, as most Americans had been looking for some definite action in retribution for the attack on Pearl Harbor.

Phil Cochran saw great potential for the new B-25H—it was easy to fly and maintain, it handled and maneuvered well at low level, and it could operate out of short airfields (as Doolittle had proved on the 450-foot deck of the *Hornet*). Apart from its 1,350-mile range and its 3,000-pound bomb-load capacity, the new aircraft had substantial armor plating for the pilots and around the fuel tanks. It was armed with eight pilot-operated, heavy machine guns in the nose and six crew-operated defensive machine guns on the top, sides, and rear; it was an ideal ground-attack aircraft.

The 1st Air Commando received twelve new aircraft and immediately modified them by installing a further sixteen pilot-operated forward firing machine guns, eight under each wing. This turned the B-25 into an incredible ground-attack weapon and the Air Commando used it to maximum advantage.

When they were fully loaded with bombs, machine-gun ammunition, and fuel, the modified craft were well over their design weight, but, apart from feeling somewhat heavy in the hands of the pilots, the sturdy craft did not seem to suffer any ill effects.

The B-25 bomber-gunships roamed over Burma, destroying bridges, trains, boats, and trucks, and in general wreaked havoc with the Japanese communications and supply lines. They attacked enemy airfields and destroyed hundreds of aircraft on the ground. After one raid of Air Commando P-51s and B-25s on the Japanese airfield near Shwebo, Royal Air Force reconnaissance photographs showed that 111 aircraft had been destroyed. Although it was not their role, the B-25s also attacked enemy aircraft in the air, with devastating results.

In conjunction with the P-51s, they drove the Japanese bomber and fighter squadrons out of their Burma bases and into New Guinea. Once that was accomplished, they turned their full attention to the task of severing all supply routes from the Japanese-held southern ports to their army in the hinterland.

In the Pacific, the task of the B-25s and the 2nd and 3rd Air Commando was somewhat different, as they did not have to support an army that was far behind enemy lines. They did, however, conduct many missions behind the lines, in conjunction with the Navy and Marine Air Wings, doing exactly what they had done in Burma—destroying the enemy's communications and supply lines.

Many B-25s are still flying today in the form of fire bombers, cargo planes, and flying test beds. A considerable number have been restored by private individuals and "flying museums," and they are flown at air shows around the country simply for nostalgia's sake.

YR-4

The *Y* designates a Service Test Model, and the *R* designates Rotorcraft, the name used before the word *helicopter* came into use.

This small, two-seat helicopter was manufactured by Sikorsky and first delivered to the Army as the XR-4 for test and evaluation in May, 1942 (*X* designated Experimental). In April, 1943, the Army ordered further improved models and the designation was changed to YR-4.

How Phil Cochran managed to persuade General Arnold to release six of the test craft for service in Burma with the Air Commando will probably never be known. The fact remains that he succeeded, and in April, 1944, the craft earned the distinction of being the first helicopter in the world both to make its appearance on the battlefield and to operate behind enemy lines.

The YR-4 had a carrying capacity of only 530 pounds—the pilot and one passenger; it had a maximum speed of seventy-five miles per hour and was incapable of going higher than eight thousand feet. It was used by the 1st Air Commando to recover wounded soldiers and aircraft crews from dense jungle areas, and as an executive transport between command posts in India.

During the later stages of the war in Europe, the Special Operations group in the Mediterranean area, under the auspices of the OSS, are known to have used YR-4s for various tasks, the most notable of which was the landing of agents in the Balkans.

The YR-4, later to become the R-4, was in service with the 1st Air Commando in Burma until the end of the war. Although there are no flying examples of this pioneering craft in existence today, one group of avid enthusiasts, the Confederate Air Force in Harlingen, Texas, hopes to restore one in the near future.

Although there were several other aircraft that saw service with the Air Commando during World War Two, those described here played the most significant roles, and they were the principal contributors to the success of this unique fighting force.

5

BATTLEFIELD LOG:
Burma Jungle—April, 1944

At the beginning of April, 1944, the British Chindits had been fighting in the jungles of Burma for almost a month since their landing at Broadway. Units of between five hundred and six hundred men had spread out in all directions from the airfield, and within three weeks some of the groups were almost eighty miles away and deep in the jungle.

The Japanese had overcome their initial surprise and confusion at the daring assault and were now fighting back with incredible ferocity. Casualties were mounting, and the Air Commando L-1s and L-5s were flying day and night—delivering supplies, guiding the P-51s and B-26s on support missions, and evacuating wounded Chindits from the jungle.

Although their craft were tiny and could carry only one passenger comfortably, the L-1 pilots would often squeeze in as many as three wounded soldiers behind them, struggle into the air from jungle clearings and river sandbars, and fly back to Broadway. When loaded with two or three wounded, the tiny craft sometimes could climb no higher than fifty feet above the treetops, and the pilots would often be forced to wind their way through valleys and gullies to get back to the airstrip. In such an overloaded condition, a small hill—no more than one hundred feet above the normal terrain—would be a major obstacle and the tiny craft would have to fly around it. Pilots carrying injured men were occasionally forced to fly forty-five to fifty miles from the rescue site to the runway at Broadway when the straight-line distance was actually no more than thirty miles.

On the morning of April 8, 1944, an L-1 was returning from a supply drop to the west of Broadway when the pilot received a call to fly to a clearing some sixty-five miles south, where three wounded Chindits were waiting to be taken to a hospital.

The Air Commando ground-control officer with the Chindits had found a perfect landing sight—a large, unobstructed clearing—and the pilot of the L-1 had no difficulty locating it and landing. The pilot was greeted in the traditional friendly manner by the Chindit soldiers and his Air Commando colleague. He discovered that his three passengers, all Englishmen, could still manage to walk, despite their wounds and extremely weak condition from loss of blood. He had intended to take two men out first and then return for the third, but the remainder of the Chindits were anxious to get away from the clearing and back into the jungle as quickly as possible. They had been in one place for too long and were very nervous—they knew that the fanatical Japanese unit they had just driven off would be regrouping and calling up reinforcements in preparation for another assault. The L-1 pilot understood their dilemma, and, since the clearing was considerably longer than most he had landed in, he offered to take all three men out at the same time, which pleased the remaining Chindits.

When all three wounded men were crammed in behind him, the pilot gunned his throttle and bounced along the clearing until he finally managed to get the grossly overloaded craft in the air. He flew over the tops of the trees at the end of the clearing with about twenty-five feet to spare, and after about twenty minutes of labored flying in the muggy jungle air he had managed to get about one hundred feet higher. That was about as high as he was going to get—the engine in the tiny craft was at full power and the L-1 had stopped climbing. He was familiar with the terrain and quickly settled in to the task of navigating around the high ground, hoping that he would not come across any stray Japanese who might decide to fire at him.

Shortly after leaving the clearing, the pilot picked up the line of a river that he knew and followed it for about thirty minutes. By taking this route he was flying in a direction away from Broadway, but he was avoiding a series of hills that his heavily laden craft could not climb over. He was also bypassing a Japanese-held area where, a week previously, he had been shot at. One round had come through the cockpit and had ripped through his trousers just above his boot, narrowly missing his leg, before tearing through the opposite side of the aircraft. He had been quite startled, since he had never been hit before or, as far as he knew, even shot at. When he realized that he had not been injured, he maneuvered the L-1 somewhat erratically for a few moments to avoid being hit a second time. His aircraft had been empty at the time, and it had not been a difficult task to sling it around. However, with three wounded men on board he could barely manage a steep turn, and he had no intention of taking a risk and inviting trouble.

After following the river for almost twenty-five minutes, he came to a series of bends—a landmark he had been waiting to see. He checked his compass heading and then slowly swung the nose of the L-1 around on a heading that would take him straight to Broadway, with the exception of a few small detours to avoid further hills. After five minutes on the new heading he located a dried-up riverbed, which was another landmark indicating that he was back over more friendly territory and some forty miles south of Broadway.

The passengers seemed to be in good spirits, despite their wounds and the cramped conditions. The pilot had just shouted back to them that they would reach the airfield in about thirty minutes when he noticed his oil-pressure gauge start to flicker a little more than usual. Five minutes later, the pressure started to fall and he felt the engine lose power. He immediately checked his position—about thirty miles south of Broadway—then radioed the airfield to inform them that he was having problems. In the event that the enemy was monitoring the frequency, he gave his estimated position in code form, then started to look around for a place to land. Although the engine was still running, he had lost a little height—about twenty-five feet—and with only one hundred feet of space between the L-1 and the treetops he knew he did not have much time.

He could not find a reasonable break in the jungle canopy to land the aircraft, and he wished he had been a little higher so that he would have been able to see farther and would have had a little more time. Suddenly he remembered that he had not informed his passengers that he was having problems and was going to have to land. As he turned around to call a warning to the wounded men, he noticed a break in a line of trees to his left and caught a faint glimpse of a small clearing just a little farther beyond. He turned toward the break in the trees, quickly telling his passengers that he was going to make a forced landing. By now the oil-pressure gauge was not moving—it was at zero, and he was rapidly losing power and altitude.

He had been hoping to find a clearing before the engine stopped, so that he would have some measure of control when he attempted to land. But he knew now that he would be lucky to get to the clearing—the engine was starting to make terrible noises and the L-1 was sinking fast. There was a loud clunking sound accompanied by a shudder and the propeller suddenly stopped turning. The vibration and clattering noise of the engine was now replaced by the rasping sound of air rushing over the fuselage. The pilot quickly went through the crash-landing procedures that his instructors had made him practice and recite out loud at least a thousand times—procedures he had hoped he would never have to use. He turned off the fuel supply and all the electrical switches. He gave his safety harness a final tug and released the catch on the door to prevent it from jamming closed during a hard landing. He hoped there would be no fire.

He cursed when he saw that the clearing was not big enough, but he thought about it only momentarily. His immediate concern was ensuring that he cleared the tops of the trees that surrounded the clearing. When the last line of trees flashed past the cockpit window, not more than a few inches below the landing gear, he heard a crashing sound that startled him, and he felt the control stick try to snatch itself from his hand. He realized instantly that the back of the L-1 had just caught the last treetop, and the already rapid descent rate seemed to accelerate as the aircraft neared the ground. The pilot eased back on the control stick, and the nose of the L-1 came up more slowly than usual because of the damage that had been done to the tail section when it hit the trees. He pulled back a little harder and the aircraft responded accordingly. The wheels hit hard, but fortunately the aircraft did not bounce back into the air.

The clearing was not quite long enough and the brakes on the L-1 were of little use. As the craft headed for the jungle scrub and trees at the end of the clearing, the pilot remembered being taught that, under such circumstances, it was best to steer the craft between the trees. By doing so it was hoped that when the wings caught on the trees, the shock would not be too severe, and there was much less likelihood of injury to the occupants or damage to the fuselage, despite the obvious rapid deceleration. Unfortunately, there was extremely dense shrubbery at the end of the clearing and the pilot could not see the tree trunks. He waited until the last possible moment and was about to turn the aircraft quickly to one side in an attempt to bring it to a stop in what is called a "ground loop" when the wheels hit a hidden rut and were almost completely torn off. The L-1 shuddered and slid on its belly and came to a stop rather quickly with its nose just sticking into the edge of the jungle.

The pilot quickly climbed out and started to drag out his unfortunate passengers. There was a danger that residual fuel would come into contact with the hot exhaust pipes and cause a fire. Fortunately, this did not occur, and neither he nor the wounded Chindits suffered anything more than a few scratches and bruises as a result of the controlled crash.

After he had helped the Chindits to safety, the pilot went back to the wreck. There was no smell of leaking fuel, and a careful examination showed that the fuel tank had not ruptured. The radio was still working and he made contact with an airborne L-5 that relayed his message to Broadway. When he had finished transmitting he went back to the Chindits and started to construct a makeshift tent with his parachute.

It was no more than thirty minutes after the crash when they heard the roar of a powerful engine and looked up to see a searching P-51 pulling around in a tight turn. The P-51 pilot had spotted the white parachute canopy from afar and was already directing an L-5 to the scene. The men on the ground waved; the P-51 pilot rocked his wings in reply and then proceeded to start a sweeping search of the area for any approaching enemy.

Shortly afterward, the L-5 appeared and dropped a survival supply pack and an extra radio. Then he, too, started a search of the area for both the enemy and a possible landing site. Apart from the almost nonexistent clearing where the L-1 had crash-landed, there was only one open area, and although it was only about a hundred yards from where the downed aircraft lay, it was not big enough to permit even an L-5 to land.

Thirty minutes of searching revealed that the nearest possible landing site was the dried-up riverbed some ten miles away; as the jungle was so dense in that area, the L-5 pilot estimated that it would take a large rescue party some two or three weeks to hack their way from the riverbed to the crash site. He relayed his findings to Colonel Cochran at Broadway, who immediately took off in a P-51 and flew over the area. He believed his L-5 pilot, but he wanted to see for himself the small clearing close to the downed men.

When Cochran reached the crash site he circled the area twice, then returned to Broadway and sent a message to the downed L-1 pilot that he would have them out within a few days.

Phil Cochran had been waiting for a suitable opportunity to justify the use of one of the new YR-4 helicopters. He had promised General Arnold that he would not risk them unnecessarily, and this, he felt, was the opportunity he had been waiting for. Cochran had not allowed the YR-4s to enter Burma. They were still undergoing service trials, and the risk of losing one unnecessarily to the enemy had been too great, but that was no longer the case. After the P-51 was refueled, he took off for Hailakandi, India.

In Hailakandi he sent for his best YR-4 pilot, Lieutenant Carter Harman, and explained the situation to him. They spent hours studying all available maps of the terrain between India and Broadway—the task of getting the YR-4 down to Broadway was not going to be easy. To start with, the Naga Mountain chain had to be crossed, and it was more than seven thousand feet high. The YR-4 had a maximum ceiling of eight thousand feet, but Lieutenant Harman had never been able to get even his best craft that high in India, and on one occasion he had nearly lost a YR-4 in the mountains at only five thousand feet in what was considered moderate turbulence by even the L-5 pilots. Also, the YR-4 had a very limited range, a little over one hundred miles, and its engine was occasionally prone to overheating.

After hours of planning, Harman and Cochran came up with a route to Broadway that was a little over six hundred miles long, almost four times the straight-line distance on the map. P-51s would escort the frail-looking YR-4 every mile of the way, and L-5s would carry extra fuel to prearranged landing sites along the route, with one exception. There was one leg of the journey over enemy-occupied jungle where the L-5s could not land, and for that section the YR-4 would carry extra fuel in a drum strapped to the passenger seat. Carter Harman would have to land, refuel the craft by himself, and then take off again. During this time the fighters would fly a protective screen overhead to keep the Japanese away.

In the event that the YR-4 was forced to land and became inoperative, Cochran instructed Harman to get clear of the craft as quickly as possible because the P-51s would destroy it. Under no circumstances could the YR-4 be allowed to fall into enemy hands.

Two days later, the YR-4 lifted off from Hailakandi with its escort of P-51s and L-5 refueling craft. Everything went well until Harman landed in the tiny jungle clearing to perform his own refueling. He was not halfway through the task when Cochran, who was leading the P-51 squadron, spotted a group of men moving through the jungle in the direction of the YR-4. He was not able to identify them clearly, but they did not look like Japanese. Suspecting that they might be inquisitive Burmese natives, he ordered the squadron to follow him on a strafing run but to confine the strike to the area in front of the potential "enemy."

Harman was busily refueling his craft and knew nothing of what was going on in the air. He admitted afterward that when he first saw the fighters swoop in his direction and then start firing he was somewhat scared. He quickly finished the refueling and lifted off, much to Cochran's relief, since he was still uncertain as to the identity of the men in the jungle.

Harman and his P-51 escorts reached Broadway just before dark, and the specialist YR-4 maintenance crew that had been flown down from India earlier in the day were waiting to inspect and service it in preparation for the forthcoming rescue mission.

The next morning, Harman took off from Broadway—again with a squadron of P-51 fighters escorting him—and flew the thirty miles south to the downed L-1.

On the journey south, Harman noticed that the steamy heat and the high altitude of the northern Burma jungle seriously affected his machine's performance. He had barely enough power to hover the craft without a passenger, and this would make life difficult for him during the rescue.

The downed L-1 pilot and his Chindit passengers had moved over to the next clearing to await the arrival of the helicopter. Harman landed the YR-4 in the clearing, to the amazement of the soldiers and the L-1 pilot. The most seriously wounded man was the first to be strapped into the helicopter for evacuation. The problem of getting the fully loaded YR-4 off the ground and out of the small clearing had been of some concern to Harman, and he had decided that he would have to try something different. As it takes considerably more power to hover any helicopter than it does to propel it in straight and level flight, Harman guessed that if he ran the engine up to full power and then suddenly jerked it off the ground, he would be able to get high enough to tilt the craft quickly into forward flight.

When he tried it the first time it worked perfectly, although from the noises he heard coming from the aircraft he knew it was quite a strain. He flew the wounded Chindit to the dried-up riverbed some ten miles to the south, where a small base camp had been set up. A waiting L-5 immediately took the soldier to the temporary hospital at Broadway, and Harman refueled and returned to the clearing to pick up the next man.

It was not as easy the second time. The air temperature had risen more than fifteen degrees since the first pickup, and the YR-4 only just made it out of the clearing. By the time he reached the riverbed, the engine was overheating badly and Harman decided not to attempt another lift, or even to fly the helicopter, until the engine had been inspected.

It was late in the evening before it had cooled down sufficiently to allow the mechanics to work on it. Fortunately, they discovered that no serious damage had been done.

As dawn broke, Harman lifted off and flew back into the clearing. Using the same technique as he had the preceding day, he lifted out the third wounded soldier and delivered him to a waiting L-5 back at the riverbed base camp. The YR-4 was refueled quickly and Harman made his last flight into the clearing to pick up the L-1 pilot. This time he did not fly back to the south; instead, he flew north to Broadway with his escort of P-51s, and during the trip he demonstrated some of the helicopter's finer points to the intrigued liaison pilot.

General Arnold was elated at the success of the operation and called for increased production and further development work with helicopters. The YR-4 designation was changed to R-4, and by the end of World War Two there were more than four hundred in service with the Army Air Corps.

6

BATTLEFIELD LOG:
Ban Karai Pass, Vietnam—
August 21, 1968

The sun was just dipping below the horizon as the AC-130 lifted off the runway at Da Nang. The takeoff run had been much longer than the pilot, Major David Cable, had expected, although he was not too surprised—the aircraft was well over its maximum rated takeoff weight, and, despite his long experience in operating the normal C-130 transport, he had never taken off with one so heavily loaded.

When he was clear of the airfield, he handed over the controls to the copilot for the journey south toward Hoi An, their assigned mission patrol area, then leaned back in his seat and relaxed. It was probably going to be a long night, much longer than usual, and Cable intended to let the copilot do as much flying as possible.

There had been two mission briefings that afternoon—the usual one for a normal night's work, then another for a special operation that they would possibly be called upon to perform. It was this special mission that had caused the AC-130 to be so heavily laden; absolute maximum fuel and more than maximum ammunition for the 20-mm and 40-mm guns had been loaded.

As he thought about his overloaded gunship and the briefing he had received for the special operation, he glanced over his shoulder and smiled at his passenger, officially called an *observer*. The man smiled in reply and held up his thumb. Cable nodded, then turned his attention back to the instrument panel.

The observer was an Army major, and David Cable assumed he was with the Special Forces, because the potential special mission, and the circumstances behind it, was the sort of thing that the Special Forces were normally involved in. However, it would be almost midnight before Cable knew if this mission was to become a reality, as final instructions were to be radioed to him later that evening.

At that time, only three people on board the gunship knew the exact location of the special mission: Major Cable, his navigating officer, and the Army major— but only the Army major knew the reason for it. The remainder of the gunship crew, who were a good-natured bunch, knew that something special was in progress, as there was almost enough ammunition on board for two gunships and it occupied so much space in the back of the aircraft that there was barely room to move. The appearance of the lean-looking, heavily armed Army officer, who had come on board with his own parachute and bulky backpack, served only to confirm the crew's suspicions that something was "going on." If they had known the real reason why the major was on board, they might have been more concerned; and even though the navigator knew the target area and thought he knew the reason why the observer was there, he had been told only part of the reason.

Apart from the Army major himself, David Cable was the only person on board who knew the truth. The major was on board the gunship for two reasons—the first (which the navigator had been told) was to assist with the actual mission. The second reason was a precautionary one, because the special mission was being carried out in the demilitarized zone close to the

North Vietnamese border. In the event that the AC-130 was hit by enemy fire and crashed-landed in North Vietnam—and there was every possibility that that could happen—the Army officer would play a vital role. Under such circumstances, his job was to ensure that the AC-130 was destroyed—a task that required an explosives expert—and then, if possible, to lead any surviving crew members to safety.

The reason for such a measure was simple: there were only four AC-130 gunships in existence, and if the special mission was called for, it would be the first time an AC-130 had operated so close to, and possibly over, North Vietnam. Some of the equipment on board the aircraft was still highly classified and the Air Force had no wish for any of it to fall into enemy hands. The bulky pack that the Army major carried was full of explosives that would be used to destroy certain parts of the aircraft, either on the ground in the event of a forced landing, or in the air after everyone bailed out.

Cable did not think much of the idea. As he had not been given any details, other than the fact that it was a support operation, he half-hoped the operation—whatever it was—would not be called. The Army major, whose name Cable had not been told, had promised that if the operation took place, he would give him a full explanation before the first shot was fired.

Cable stopped thinking about what might or might not happen, as he and his crew had other work to do, some almost immediately. The first task was a gun and system check. Accurate alignment of the side-firing guns with the gunsight by Cable's left shoulder was vital. An initial "bore sighting" and sensing-equipment calibration check was always performed on the ground before takeoff, but a live firing test had to be conducted to fine-tune the system. There was no point in arriving at the target area to discover that while the target-data acquisition and processing were giving correct firing information, the guns and the gunsight were not synchronized and aligned properly.

The navigator called that they were two minutes from the site chosen for the test firing, and Cable took control of the gunship. On the first orbit of the target all the guns were test-fired and a few minor adjustments were required. Although it was not really necessary, Cable pulled out of the target-orbiting attitude and flew straight and level for a few moments as the calibration adjustments were made.

When the fire-control officer, sitting at the control console just behind and to the right of Cable, informed him that the corrections were made, he swung the gunship around and approached the target again. As he settled the huge craft into the left-hand orbit, he looked through the gunsight and picked up the target. The copilot called out the speed and altitude as the aircraft circled, and Cable fired each gun in turn. The adjustments had corrected the errors of the first test, and both Cable and the fire-control officer, who was responsible for accurate target identification before any gun could be fired, were satisfied. The guns were made safe. Cable then handed control of the gunship back to his copilot for the remainder of the trip to their assigned patrol area near Hoi An.

The test firing had been watched with interest by the Army major, and when the fire-control officer asked him what he thought about it he replied, "Impressive."

They were approaching their loiter area over Hoi An when a call came for air support from a small hamlet about twenty miles south of the town. Less than a minute after the call was received, the navigator finished plotting the course to the hamlet and gave it to Cable. The copilot, on instructions from Cable, had already brought the gunship around onto an approximate heading and had eased the throttles forward to increase speed. Only minor alterations were needed to bring the aircraft onto the navigator's plot, and Cable called out the new speed setting. Moments later the navigator called out, "Three minutes and ten seconds to target."

The gun crew went back to their stations, and the ramp at the rear of the gunship was lowered. The illuminator operator, whose primary responsibility was the management of the flare launchers and the powerful searchlight mounted at the rear of the gunship, was also responsible for watching for anti-aircraft fire (called "Triple A".) In order to do this, he would walk out to the end of the open rear ramp wearing a safety harness with a steel cable firmly attached to it; the other end was attached to an anchor point inside the aircraft. He would then lie down on the edge of the ramp, from where he had an excellent field of view below the gunship, and keep a lookout for enemy-anti-aircraft fire.

With the nature of anti-aircraft fire being such that the shells are set to explode at a predetermined altitude and discharge shrapnel in all directions, the illuminator operator, hanging over the edge of the ramp, would clearly see the burst patterns. He would then call evasive instructions to the pilot. Although it sounds somewhat primitive, it is to this day one of the most effective methods a gunship has of avoiding areas that anti-aircraft guns are saturating with fire (more usually called "flak").

As they neared the hamlet they could clearly see that a firefight was in progress on the ground from the occasional flares that were being fired aloft by the defenders. They radioed the Army unit on the ground to announce their arrival overhead, and the officer in charge of the ground forces called for illumination and suppressive fire at the northeast corner of the tiny hamlet.

Cable brought the gunship around on a flare drop and released two flares, which swathed the area with an eerie light. A large group of the enemy could be seen moving close to the buildings at the edge of the village. As Cable maneuvered the gunship into an attack position, the fire-control officer asked the Army officer on the ground for a safe zone. The reply came quickly, and within seconds the fire-control officer confirmed the target acquisition and authorized Cable to fire.

He fired a cautionary two-second burst from the number-one 20-mm Vulcan gun and watched the tracers find their mark. Satisfied, he opened up with both Vulcans in a series of three-second bursts, compensating for the outward swing of the gunship's nose as the cannons generated a slight sideways thrust. He saw the tracers fan out over the target area, and in the light of the flares the enemy could now be seen breaking cover and retreating from the edge of the hamlet.

Cable readjusted his aim away from the buildings and the fire-control officer confirmed the change as a matter of routine. This time he selected one of the rear 40-mm Bofors guns, which had a wider field of fire, and released about twenty rounds. He then went back to one of the Vulcan cannons for a further series of three-second bursts.

The ground commander called and informed them that the threat on that side of the hamlet had diminished, but a further group of mixed Vietcong and North Vietnamese regulars was creeping up under cover of fairly dense shrub on the southwest side. The first flares were dying, so Cable called for two more to be launched as he moved into position over the new target area.

The second set of flares fired before the first ones fully extinguished, and shortly afterward the fire-control officer confirmed the target zone on the southwest side. Cable opened up again with one 20-mm gun in a two-second burst and followed it almost immediately with a series of five-second bursts from both guns. Through breaks in the undergrowth the enemy could be seen pulling back from the hamlet, and the Bofors gun was brought into action for several short bursts.

From his windy position on the rear of the ramp, the illuminator operator had seen no anti-aircraft fire, but he had an excellent view of the effects of the chattering

Vulcan cannons and the steady *thud-thud* of the slower-firing Bofors. He was just starting to feel cold when he heard the call to secure the guns, and he pulled himself back off the ramp. The commander of the small garrison had called to say that the enemy fire had ceased and the enemy could be heard retreating. The immediate threat was now over, but the enemy was not necessarily giving up—they would probably wait to hear the gunship leave the area and then start the assault again.

Cable decided to try to lure them back and asked the ground commander for the speed and direction of the surface winds. When he received a reply he conferred with the navigator, who confirmed the numbers, as he had been watching the flares falling. The wind speed at the gunship's altitude was somewhat higher and coming from a slightly different direction, which was quite a normal occurrence. Further calculations by the navigator produced a course that would take them away from the hamlet in a downwind direction. Cable handed control of the aircraft to the copilot for the decoy trip and informed the defenders of the hamlet that they would not be far away.

About an hour later they received a call from the hamlet to say that the enemy had started to attack again. The deception had worked, and minutes later the gunship was back in action, first with the flares and then with the 20-mm and 40-mm guns. The enemy was obviously serious about taking the hamlet, and Cable radioed for heavier striking power.

Twenty minutes later, an A-1 Skyraider carrying napalm and fragmentation bombs arrived in the area, and the gunship adopted the role of forward air controller and flareship. With the use of his aircraft's sophisticated sensing equipment, Cable directed the A-1 pilot to the largest concentration of the enemy forces. Within minutes after his arrival at the hamlet the A-1 pilot had dropped almost eight tons of ordnance on the enemy and had made several strafing runs with his miniguns blazing.

*   *   *

Shortly after the A-1 had left, Cable received a message that they were being replaced by an AC-47 Spooky gunship and that he was to proceed at once northeast to the A Shau Valley in Thua Thien Province. An enemy supply column, consisting of some seventeen trucks, had been reported en route from Laos and was presently crossing the border into South Vietnam. Cable was ordered to hunt for the trucks and destroy them if possible.

The aging but still effective AC-47 arrived in the area some fifteen minutes later, and, after almost three and a half hours over the hamlet, the AC-130 set course for the A Shau Valley.

On the way there, Cable watched the moon come up and commented to the Army major, who was also watching, that it had a greenish hue to it. He saw a strange-looking smile come to the major's face as he nodded in agreement; after a brief silence, he informed Cable that it was to their benefit since most of the North Vietnamese soldiers believed an old legend that the green moon was an omen of bad things to come. Cable shrugged his shoulders; he did not think much about such fairy tales and he found it hard to believe that the Army major did either—however, it had certainly been a bad night for the attackers of the hamlet.

It was shortly after 2300 hours when the sensors detected truck movement on a narrow road near A Shau, and shortly afterward a count of seventeen vehicles was established. Cable took control of the gunship and started an orbit on the lead vehicle of the convoy. The fire-control officer signaled that everything was in order, and Cable opened up with the 40-mm Bofors. He saw the shells strike, and moments later a secondary explosion confirmed that he had hit the lead truck. He quickly pulled the gunship out of the orbit and repositioned it over the last truck in the convoy. Again the fire-control officer confirmed the target and Cable pressed the firing button for the Bofors. This truck took a few more rounds than the first one before it burst into flames. Cable immediately called for flares. When they ignited, the convoy could be clearly seen, neatly sandwiched between the burning lead and tail trucks.

"Targets at your discretion, sir," called the fire-control officer, and Cable set to work at what he enjoyed most—destroying enemy trucks. Within minutes, almost three-quarters of the convoy was ablaze and he broke off the attack. He brought the gunship into level flight and signaled the copilot to change seats with him. He quickly switched on the automatic pilot, and the seat exchange took less than ten seconds to complete. The delighted copilot strapped himself into the captain's seat, released the auto pilot, and brought the aircraft back over the blazing convoy. The fire-control officer smiled as he gave him the signal to fire at will, and the copilot went to work on the remaining vehicles.

Although not as adept as his captain, he finished off the remaining trucks in the convoy without wasting too much ammunition, except for the final truck, which he obliterated with a long burst from the Bofors.

As they pulled away from the trail littered with wrecked and blazing trucks, Cable reported the success of the mission to their headquarters. After a brief congratulatory messsage he was given instructions to loiter slightly farther to the north and to seek "targets of opportunity." He remained in the copilot's seat to give the younger pilot a chance to initiate an action of his own while, he busied himself by writing down brief details of the action against the convoy.

Cable was still in the copilot's seat and had almost forgotten about the special mission when he heard the coded message coming through his earphones. He immediately glanced at the Army major, who was also wearing a headset, and saw no trace of emotion on his face. The message was acknowledged by the navigator, who immediately started to plot a course for Ho Village in the demilitarized zone between North and South Vietnam.

The major stood up and handed a sealed envelope to Cable. When he had read it he shook his head and then handed it to the navigator. Cable saw the surprised look on the navigator's face as he glanced from the letter to the charts on the plotting table in front of him. They were not going to an area south of Ho Village, they were going much farther to the north, to the Ban Karai Pass area—a considerable distance into North Vietnam.

As the navigator plotted the new course, the Army major explained to Cable the reason for the mission. The area around Ban Karai Pass was what was known as a "Main Gate," a narrow, all-weather pass or road through a mountain range that the enemy supply columns were compelled to negotiate on their way south to Laos, Cambodia, or South Vietnam. Recent intelligence information had indicated that a little to the north of Ban Karai the enemy was amassing a considerable army and had built up a huge supply base in preparation for a major offensive in the south.

For almost three weeks, one of the major's special reconnaissance teams had steadily worked their way to the pass area and had found the enemy encampment. They had spent a further week making a detailed survey of the enemy's disposition and had radioed most of the information back to their operations headquarters. As a result, a major aerial bombardment had been planned as soon as the team got clear of the area. Unfortunately, in their attempts to get to safety the team had been discovered by the enemy. With some remarkable luck they had managed to avoid capture, despite the fact that two members of the team had been wounded in the firefight. They had made several further attempts to leave the area, but with wounded men and the surrounding territory crowded with enemy soldiers, it was proving to be an almost impossible task.

Time was now running out for the air attack—further intelligence reports indicated that within a few days the enemy would move most of their troops down into South Vietnam. The stranded team leader had requested permission to make one final attempt to lead his men clear of the area and had suggested that the bombing should take place regardless of the outcome.

One daylight and one nighttime attempt had been made using helicopters with a fixed wing escort, but they had ended in near disaster as the helicopters had spent too much time searching for the reconnaissance team. As a result, it had been decided that the relatively new AC-130, with its sophisticated sensing equipment and tremendous firepower, would be commited to the rescue, providing that adequate measures were taken to ensure that the gunship did not fall into enemy hands.

The reconnaissance team had in their possession a small radio beacon that operated on an extremely "discreet" frequency, and the Air Force was more than confident that the AC-130 could guide a rescue helicopter directly to the beacon. The officers who planned the rescue mission were also confident that the gunship could provide accurate and continuous suppressive fire in close proximity to the rescue craft—which was to be the fast CH-3 helicopter—when it landed to pick up the reconnaissance team. The complete operation would have to be performed in one fast run, otherwise both gunship and helicopter would certainly sustain damage.

The reconnaissance-team leader was informed of the operation and was asked to find a suitable location, preferably on the top of a small hill that was clear of nearby hills that were higher. This was requested in order to avoid the possibility of the enemy shooting down onto the top of the CH-3, where it was somewhat more vulnerable, and to enable the gunship to ring the area with fire.

The team leader had said that he had in mind a location that he would like to try to reach. However, he pointed out that getting there would take almost eight hours, and then there was the infinite possibility that they would be discovered in the attempt. The rescue planners accepted the team leader's location and he was instructed to move as darkness fell the next day.

At about the time the reconnaissance team was preparing to move, David Cable was lifting off the runway at Da Nang. He had been directed to fly south and engage in normal operations in order to avoid suspicion from everpresent enemy eyes. While he was destroying the truck convoy, the rescue planners received a call from the team leader to say that they had made good time and were now on the appointed hill.

Cable now moved back into his own seat and set course for a rendezvous with the CH-3 north of Khe Sanh. When they made contact, they moved closer to the demilitarized zone and a message was sent to the reconnaissance team to turn on the beacon for a reference check. The gunship's sensors picked up the signal almost immediately, and ten seconds later Cable instructed that the beacon be turned off; although it was unlikely, he did not want to take a chance of the enemy somehow locating the beacon.

When courses and speeds had been plotted, Cable sent the helicopter on a low, fast run to the north. From their position above the helicopter, the gunship's sensor operators tracked it without difficulty. Intending to guide the rescue craft from behind until it neared the hilltop, Cable held his position as the helicopter moved north. He would then use the AC-130's greater speed to arrive over the location at the same time as the CH-3.

When the giant helicopter was well over North Vietnam, Cable called for the beacon to be turned on permanently. Shortly afterward, a shout from the fire-control officer informed him that the beacon had been picked up again. At that point he opened the throttles and started to chase the CH-3.

As the gunship started to close on the helicopter, the navigator called course corrections to keep the rescue craft "straight down the beam." This procedure continued slowly at first, but became more rapid as the distance to the target became less and minor piloting errors caused greater divergence from the beacon's guiding rays. When they were about ten miles from the beacon the navigator instructed Cable to slow down a little—there was a chance he would overshoot the CH-3 before they reached the beacon.

When the reconnaissance team heard the helicopter in the distance, the team leader prepared his tiny signal light to provide final guidance to their position. He did not need to do so, however, as the gunship was already calling off the distance to the beacon to the CH-3 pilot. When it was within one hundred yards of the hilltop the copilot of the helicopter spotted the team and yelled a warning to his pilot. The CH-3 seemed to rear up on its tail as the pilot quickly slowed it down. As he started to descend onto the hill, Cable swung the gunship into a firing orbit overhead.

Almost immediately, enemy fire came from the lower slopes of the hill. Cable opened up in reply with both 20-mm Vulcans in a spectacular and devastating ten-second burst. As the gunship's tracers lit the sky, the CH-3's wheels touched the ground and four men came stumbling in a huddled group under the swirling rotors. When they reached the helicopter's open door, two of the men literally threw the other two into the helicopter before the crew chief could get his hands on them.

The two soldiers then turned and raced back out under the rotors into the darkness; moments later they returned, carrying rifles and heavy packs, which they slung inside the helicopter. Then they both scrambled in and one of them signaled the crew chief to lift off.

As they lifted off the hilltop they saw a downpour of vivid, orange-red 20-mm tracers streaking out of the sky to fan out along the sides of the hill. Cable had been pouring the fire down from both the Vulcan cannons, in ten-second bursts, since the helicopter had touched down on the hilltop.

The CH-3 pilot radioed the gunship and told Cable

that he had the reconnaissance team on board. He then asked for a safe exit from the hilltop as he was afraid of running into the almost blinding tracer fire. As the gunship's navigator gave him an exit line, Cable changed to the 40-mm Bofors and continued to fire in a series of long bursts until the helicopter was well clear of the hilltop.

According to the CH-3 pilot, he had been on top of the hill for only fifty-two seconds but it had seemed more like fifty-two minutes. The AC-130 had fired almost eleven thousand rounds into the hill during that brief interlude, and neither craft had sustained hits from enemy ground fire.

The CH-3 took the reconnaissance team back to their own base camp, but the gunship was not finished—it still had ample fuel and ammunition left. For several more hours Cable and his crew flew random "seek and destroy" patterns in the southwest corner of Quang Tri Province and added another eight trucks to their list of kills.

The copilot was flying the gunship in a westerly direction when Cable yawned and looked at his watch. As he did so, the illuminator operator, who was looking out over the open ramp to the east, called and asked him if he had heard the noise. Cable smiled and asked, "What noise?"

"The crack of dawn, sir," came the reply.

Cable laughed, despite the fact that he had heard it said many times. "Okay," he said, "let's go home. This baby doesn't like the light."

7

PRINCIPAL AIRCRAFT OF THE AIR COMMANDO DURING THE VIETNAM WAR

As far as Air Commando operations are concerned, there was a great similarity between the war in the jungles of Burma and the war in the jungles of Vietnam. One of the first Air Commando aircraft to see service in Vietnam was the venerable C-47 transport, which was, by then, the oldest serving aircraft in the Air Force inventory.

During the early days of the war the C-47 was engaged in its customary role of general cargo, supply, and troop transporter, but as the war progressed the ubiquitous C-47 was to become one of the most devastating and unusual air–ground support weapons in the history of military aviation.

AC-47
The Vietnam conflict was a guerrilla war that produced mission requirements that the U.S. Air Force was not fully equipped to handle. The most obvious discrepancy was their inability to provide adequate air support to isolated troop positions, Marine Corps and Army long-

range reconnaissance patrols, small fortified towns, and forward air bases. These groups were often subject to attacks from both small enemy raiding parties and full battalion-strength units.

Fighters and fighter bombers functioned reasonably well in the air–ground support role during daylight hours, but they were hindered because they had neither the ammunition- nor fuel-carrying capacity to loiter in the target area for extended periods of time. During the hours of darkness, little or no air support was possible because problems with target identification and illumination made operations extremely hazardous, for both the aircraft and the friendly forces on the ground. The situation became serious when the enemy realized that they could simply wait for darkness to fall, when the aircraft would return to their base, before they mounted a major attack.

The obvious solution was an aircraft that could loiter for extended periods, and that had sufficient and accurate fire power and the capacity to provide adequate illumination for both itself and any other specialist aircraft that might be called upon to assist.

The Air Commando C-47s had been deployed as flareships and they had demonstrated their ability both to accurately illuminate an area and to loiter. With typical Air Commando ingenuity, Captain Ronald Terry finally persuaded the Air Force to try mounting side-firing machine guns in the C-47. Experiments were conducted with as many as ten fixed windows and doors of the aircraft. The pilot would put his aircraft into a left-hand turn around the target and fire the guns. This idea worked quite well, but the Air Commando was not satisfied and continued to experiment.

The result was the mounting of three 7.62-mm Gatling-type guns, known as *miniguns*, in the left side of the C-47. A conventional gunsight was installed at the window near the pilot's left shoulder and a firing trigger was mounted on the aircraft's control wheel. As he flew the aircraft in a left turn, the pilot could aim and fire any of the guns or all three guns at the same time.

Each gun had a possible rate of fire of six thousand rounds per minute; thus, the pilot had at his fingertips the awesome capability of delivering eighteen thousand rounds per minute at any given target. No pilot would keep the trigger pressed for a full minute—apart from the damage it could do by overheating the gun barrels, it was almost never required. Accurately fired bursts of one to five seconds with all three guns in operation produced an unbelievable amount of devastation, and to harried U.S. soldiers it was a sight to behold.

Apart from their miniguns and a considerable supply of ammunition they also carried forty-five large parachute flares for illumination during night operations.

After initial tests with a single aircraft under combat conditions proved incredibly successful, twenty C-47 gunships—redesignated AC-47s—were assigned to the 4th Air Commando Squadron. They were immediately nicknamed Spooky because of the feeling they evoked when they were first seen in action. As a result, all future Air Force gunships were given names that began with the letter S—Stinger, Shadow, Spectre, and so on.

Anyone who has ever seen an AC-47 operating at close quarters will confirm that it is a strange feeling to see the docile old C-47 spit fire, smoke, and bullets like a raging dragon. It did not take long before they became known as Puff the Magic Dragon, or, more simply, Dragonships. They were overwhelmingly successful and were used for a wide range of operations— air–ground support, armed reconnaissance patrols, airfield-perimeter defense, land-convoy escorts, and interdiction missions against enemy supply columns on the Ho Chi Minh Trail.

Watching the AC-47s in operation in Vietnam almost gave one the feeling that they were taking revenge for all the shots that had ever been fired at them during the more than twenty years they had been unarmed. They became the forerunners of a breed of mighty gunships and, once again, they started a new chapter in the history of aerial warfare.

AC-119

This large, twin-engined transport aircraft, manufactured by the Fairchild Engine and Aircraft Corporation, had a top speed of 218 miles per hour and was called the Flying Boxcar. It was first produced in 1950 and saw notable service during the Korean War.

Because of the success of the aging AC-47 and the demand for bigger and more heavily armed gunships, this aircraft was chosen for modification by the Air Commando. In December, 1968, the first of these huge gunships, designated the AC-119G Shadow and armed with four 7.62-mm miniguns, arrived at Nha Trang Air Base in South Vietnam. They were an immediate success and further aircraft were ordered to replace the tired AC-47s. In October, 1969, thirteen AC-119K Stinger aircraft were delivered to Phan Rang Air Base. These K models were jet-power assisted and, as well as the four 7.62-mm miniguns, they carried two 20-mm cannons.

By the end of 1969 there were twenty-nine AC-119 Shadow and Stinger gunships in operation, and all but three of the pioneering AC-47s had been withdrawn from service.

AC-130

The C-130 Hercules transport was manufactured by the Lockheed Aircraft Corporation and first saw service in 1958. This four-engined turboprop aircraft had a cruising speed of 375 miles per hour and could carry a payload of almost thirty-six hundred pounds.

During the Vietnam War it was a "top of the line" transport aircraft, but because of the success of the AC-47s, the Air Commando was given four of the craft to be converted into gunships. In September, 1967, before the advent of the AC-119 Shadow, these four AC-130 Gunship IIs were operating in Laos. They were armed with four 7.62-mm miniguns and four 20-mm cannons and they had improved gunsights. They were capable of carrying an incredible amount of ammunition and they could remain airborne all day long.

As the C-130 was one of the best transport aircraft in the Air Force inventory, it was decided that further aircraft could not be committed to the Air Commando and the decision was made to convert the C-119s.

Late in 1970 the Air Force released further C-130s for modification, and by 1971 there were eighteen AC-130s, now called Spectres, in operation. Some of the later models now had 40-mm cannons installed, as well as the usual complement of miniguns. There were other improvements in the form of advanced sensor systems and computerized target-acquisition systems.

The AC-130 Spectre was the most incredible of the gunships and it became the finest "truck killer" of the war, among other things.

The AC-47 Spooky and the AC-119 Shadow and Stinger were awesome to watch in action, night or day, but the AC-130 Spectre was almost unbelievable and was, without question, the most successful tactical air weapon of the entire war.

C-123

This twin-engined, propeller-driven aircraft was manufactured by Fairchild in 1954 and was originally designed as a large transport glider. It had a cruising speed of 205 miles per hour, had long-range capability, and was an excellent short-takeoff and -landing aircraft. It was because of its ability to carry more than twenty-four thousand pounds of cargo and operate from small, rough airstrips that it was acquired by the Air Commando for transport duties in counterinsurgency operations.

The C-123 saw considerable service as a general-purpose cargo-and-troop carrier, in and out of remote jungle areas, and it was also used to drop paratroopers and cargo into areas that were not accessible even to helicopters.

The addition of small, jet-booster engines, mounted

on pylons beneath the wings, gave the C-123 even greater short-field-takeoff capability, and it was an impressive sight to see a fully laden C-123 take off in a few hundred feet from a rough airstrip.

Toward the end of the war a few C-123s were converted into gunships for special night operations and were designated AC-123Ks.

O-1

The O-1E (O designates Observation), called the Bird Dog, was a high-wing, two-seat, single-engine, propeller-driven aircraft with a top speed of 130 miles per hour. It was designed and built after World War Two by the Cessna Aircraft Company, in response to an Army Air Force request for a more modern Liaison/Observation craft to replace the valiant L-1s and L-5s. The O-1, like its predecessor, the L-5, could be quickly converted to carry a stretcher by the removal of the seat behind the pilot.

Production-line aircraft entered service with the Army Air Force in December, 1950, with the designation L-19A Bird Dog, and it saw limited action in the Korean War. It was redesignated the O-1 in 1962 and was obtained by the U.S Air Force for service as a forward air controller in Vietnam. Hard points were installed beneath the wings and 2.75 smoke rockets were installed and used to mark targets for the strike aircraft.

They were ideally suited to the purpose of the Air Commando and were used extensively as forward air controllers for the fearsome gunships and various other strike and attack aircraft. They would often be sent out on random scouting and patrolling missions, and if they came across any enemy forces they would call up the strike aircraft and then loiter in the area to guide them onto the target with their smoke rockets. If Army or Marine artillery was nearby, they would call the coordinates to the gunners and then act as spotters and call the necessary corrections until the shells were falling on target.

On numerous occasions they acted as radio relay stations for the Marine and Army long-range reconnaissance patrols that operated far inside enemy-held territory. The Air Commando O-1 pilots were often called upon by the same patrols to get them out of trouble when they were being hunted down by enemy ground forces.

Although they were withdrawn from service at the end of the Vietnam War, there are scores of privately owned Bird Dogs still flying, and many of them are still put to good use with the volunteer search-and-rescue organization, the Civil Air Patrol.

O-2

In their search for a more effective forward air-control aircraft for use in Vietnam, the Air Force chose this unusual high-winged, propeller-driven, twin-engined Cessna aircraft, straight "off the shelf." It had a side-by-side pilot and copilot seating arrangement, which is what the Air Force and Air Commando were looking for. Experience in Vietnam with the tandem seat arrangement in the O-1 had shown that, under critical conditions, the pilot's effectiveness as an observer, navigator, and forward air controller was somewhat reduced due to the concentration required to fly the aircraft. Side-by-side seating would allow a copilot/navigator/observer to be carried who would have the same forward visibility as the pilot, but not the responsibility of flying the aircraft.

The Cessna 337 Skymaster was unusual because it was a "push-pull" configuration. One engine, the pull, was mounted on the nose of the fuselage, and the other, the push, was attached to the back of the main cabin. The tail section was mounted behind the fuselage on twin booms, which were attached to the rear of the wings on either side of the push engine. Cessna produced this four-to-six-passenger aircraft as the Model

337 Skymaster in 1965, after several years of development. It had a maximum speed of 206 miles per hour and was an extremely easy aircraft to fly, even if one engine became inoperative. This is not always the case with more conventional twin-engined aircraft, where the engines are mounted on either side of the fuselage, because in the event of an engine failure the aircraft would immediately start to swing violently to whichever side the dead engine was on.

Technically this is known as an asymmetric flight condition, but simply stated it means that there is a serious imbalance situation, as the dead engine acts like a powerful air brake on just one side of the aircraft, and this is what causes the swing or adverse yaw condition. Not only is the pilot faced with the problem of his aircraft trying to turn violently to one side, but he has to contend with the fact that he has lost half his power. Under such conditions, it takes a considerable amount of skill to prevent the aircraft from getting into further difficulties and sinking rapidly toward the ground. The Air Force was well aware of the fact that most accidents in conventional twin-engined aircraft occurred as a result of one engine's failing. As the mission role of forward air-control aircraft is almost always performed at low altitudes, an engine failure could prove fatal. Because of this, the Air Force considered that a conventional twin-engined craft was not worth the risk, and they chose the Cessna 337 Skymaster because the engines were "in-line" and potential problems with asymmetric flight control did not exist.

The 337 became the O-2 Milirole and first saw service in Vietnam in 1967. There were two versions, the O-2A, which was fitted with smoke-rocket launchers, flare dispensers, and 7.62-mm minigun pods. The O-2B was used for psychological warfare and was fitted with a powerful air-to-ground broadcasting system using three six-hundred-watt amplifiers and an array of directional speakers, as well as a leaflet-dispensing system. Both models were equipped with advanced navigation and communications equipment.

During extensive operations in Vietnam the O-2 Milirole saw valuable service with the Air Commando and completely justified its selection. It is still in use in limited numbers with the Air Force, although not with the Air Commando/Special Operations Wings.

A-26

This twin-engined World War Two light bomber was manufactured by Douglas Aircraft and first saw service in 1944. It was originally designated the A-26 by the Army Air Force but was then redesignated the B-26 in 1948 after the formation of the U.S. Air Force.

After extensive service in Korea it was scheduled to be removed from the Air Force inventory, but the advent of the Vietnam crisis delayed its relegation.

Extensive modifications were performed to turn it into a special Counterinsurgency Operations (COIN) aircraft in 1963 and it was once again redesignated, back to A-26. It had a top speed of about 370 miles per hour and was heavily armed, normally with eight .50-caliber (12.7-mm) machine guns in the nose and rocket pods underneath the wings. It could also carry at least six thousand pounds of bombs on hard points and pylons beneath the wings. However, the Air Commando, which never seem satisfied with any aircraft's standard armament, did modify their A-26s further and additional guns and rockets were added to a number of the aircraft.

The A-26A was used primarily in the night interdiction role, operating over Laos, Cambodia, and North Vietnam. They attacked everything from troops to supply bases and even river traffic, but they specialized in destroying trucks on the Ho Chi Minh Trail, among other places. They would often fly joint missions with other aircraft, particularly the AC-47 Spooky, and between them they could really create havoc with the enemy's supply lines.

By 1969 the A-26 was becoming hard to keep in the

air, attrition and lack of spare parts being the main problems, and the Invader was withdrawn from Air Force operational service.

A-1

Designed for the U.S. Navy during World War Two, this aircraft, called the Skyraider, did not enter operational service until the war was over. It was the largest propeller-driven, single-engine, single-seat fighter bomber ever built, and it was used extensively, with considerable success, during the Korean War.

Although there were many variants of this incredible aircraft, only two versions were used by the Air Commando: the A-1E, which carried two pilots (Navy AD-5); and the A-1H and A-1J, which were single-seat aircraft (Navy AD-7).

The A-1E had a top speed of 270 miles per hour and was armed with four 20-mm cannons, which were mounted in the wings. In its utility configuration it could carry about one ton of cargo inside the fuselage, which could be air-dropped through a hatch in the floor; or, instead of cargo, it could carry eight fully equipped paratroopers, who would also exit through the floor hatch. With no cargo or passengers on board it could carry up to four tons of ordnance, usually a mixture of napalm, bombs, and rockets, on fifteen wing pylons.

The larger-engined A1J single-seater had a maximum speed of 320 miles per hour and could carry almost seven tons of bombs, more than the four-engined B-17 bomber of World War Two fame. It was also armed with 20-mm wing cannons and was occasionally modified to carry minigun pods and rockets for ground-support operations. With the addition of long-range fuel tanks, the A-1 could remain airborne for almost ten hours, an impossible task for the high-speed jet attack aircraft, without air-to-air refueling. It was nicknamed the Spad, after the famous World War One fighter, and it became one of the most versatile and hardworked fighter bombers of the Vietnam War.

The Skyraider is still ı. ¬ervice with various emerging nations, and a few priv₂ ₂ly owned aircraft are still being flown for pleasure by their enthusiastic owners.

A-37
Called the Dragonfly, this was the first official jet aircraft to see service with the Air Commando. It was a two-seat, side-by-side twin-engined aircraft, originally designed at the hands of the Air Commando pilots in 1967, and was in operation until the end of the Vietnam conflict. Because of its somewhat limited endurance, it was used mostly as a close air-support fighter for ground forces and was extremely effective in that role.

The A-37 Dragonfly is still in service with the Air Force, although not with the Special Operations Squadrons, and with the Air National Guard. It is also in use with the Thai Air Force and with the armed forces of several South American nations.

U-10
This remarkable little single-engined aircraft was first ordered as the L-28 and was later redesignated the U-10. It was classed as a short takeoff and landing (STOL), communications, and utility aircraft, and could carry up to eight passengers or almost three-quarters of a ton of cargo. It had a top speed of about 170 miles per hour, but more important to the Air Commando was the fact that it had a slow-speed capability of only 30 miles per hour and could land on a rough field in fewer than 270 feet.

It was ideally suited for jungle work and was used extensively for clandestine operations, particularly with the Army Special Forces for infiltration, exfiltration, and supply. One of the supply-drop techniques was to fly at treetop height until the drop position was reached, at which point the pilot would suddenly pull the aircraft up to about two hundred feet above the ground, release his precious cargo, and then immediately dive back down to treetop height. The use of this technique gave a watching enemy little or no time to accurately locate the position of the Special Forces' reconnaissance patrols.

The U-10 was occasionally armed with machine guns or rocket pods for special missions or surprise attacks on small enemy camps, and it was also used as a PSYOPS craft for broadcasting and leaflet-dropping in enemy-held territory. A few of these remarkable STOL craft are still in use with the Air National Guard and the U.S. Army, and a considerable number of them are being used by the armed forces of several smaller nations and as "bush planes" by numerous civilian companies.

AT-28

Called the Trojan, this aircraft was originally manufactured in 1952 by the North American Aircraft Corporation as a trainer for the U.S. Navy and Air Force and was designated the T-28. This large, tandem two-seat, single-engine, propeller-driven aircraft was converted to a ground-attack aircraft for use in Vietnam in 1962 because of its load-carrying capacity and its manueverability. It was later designated the AT-28 and was used extensively as a fighter bomber. It had a top speed of about 340 miles per hour and was armed with a variety of machine-gun pods and rockets. It could also carry almost two tons of bombs and napalm on six underwing hard points and was an extremely reliable aircraft.

The AT-28 and T-28 Trojan are no longer in service with the Air Force, but they are still being used by South American, Asian, and French armed forces, and a considerable number of privately owned aircraft are currently flying in Europe and the United States.

CH-3C

Otherwise known as the Big Charlie or Jolly Green Giant, several versions of this helicopter were used by the Air Commando for counterinsurgency airlift purposes.

A variant of the Sikorsky S-61 aircraft, it had a top speed of about 160 miles per hour. It was armed with two 7.62-mm minigun pods and could carry some twenty-five fully armed troops or almost four tons of cargo. It was used extensively in Special Warfare civic-action operations, such as evacuating refugees and airlifting medical teams and food supplies into remote villages. It was also used to rescue downed pilots and to exfiltrate Special Forces and reconnaissance patrols from behind enemy lines in emergency situations.

It is still in service with the Air Force although it is no longer used by the Air Commando Special Operations Squadron.

UH-1

Probably the most well known of all the helicopters operating during the Vietnam crisis, the UH-1 was almost always referred to as the Huey, and was used in large numbers by both the Army and the Marines.

Manufactured in several versions by Bell Helicopters, it had a top speed of about 150 miles per hour and could carry six to eight passengers or about one ton of cargo. It was used by the Air Commando, normally unarmed, in a similar role to that of the CH-3, and a more modern version is still in use with the Special Operations Wings.

8
BATTLEFIELD LOG:
South Vietnam—February, 1969

The AC-119 gunships first arrived at Nha Trang Air Force base in South Vietnam, in the hands of pilots of the 71st Special Operations Squadron, on December 17, 1968. Shortly after their arrival they were in action against the Vietcong and North Vietnamese regulars. With much greater firepower and somewhat more sophisticated equipment than Spooky, they caused considerable havoc among the enemy troops.

The Air Force decided to assign the name *Creep* to the AC-119, because of the capabilities it had with its sophisticated equipment. The officers and men of the 71st Squadron, however, were horrified when they heard of the assignment, and they protested so vehemently—almost to a mutinous level—that the senior Air Force commanders who had authorized the name withdrew it. They then accepted and assigned the name selected by the men of the squadron—the Shadow—as it was in keeping with the "S" designation of its fellow gunships, Spooky and Spectre.

The 71st Squadron was only in service in Vietnam from January 5 to June 1, 1969, less than six months. During that short time they built themselves quite a reputation in the air–ground support role, despite the fact that the AC-119 was rather slow, difficult to maneuver, and very vulnerable to enemy ground fire.

By June 1 the 71st Squadron had flown a total of 1,209 missions, and had engaged the enemy in almost sixteen hundred individual incidents during those missions. That amounted to over six thousand hours of combat flying time, in which they killed nearly two thousand enemy troops and destroyed some fifty-one vehicles. In performing their missions they used fourteen million rounds of ammunition, which might seem like a large amount, but is actually very conservative for such a heavily armed gunship.

In their normal air–ground support role, the 71st Squadron saved the lives of countless soldiers and civilians when they assisted in driving off relentless Vietcong attackers from towns, hamlets, and outposts. However, they were to become more famous for saving the life of one single unknown soldier than for anything else that they did.

Late one evening, a small Army Special Forces and Republic of Vietnam training camp came under attack from a mixed group of Vietcong and North Vietnamese regulars. During the savage firefight that ensued, the enemy were driven back again and again by the Special Forces and the well-trained South Vietnamese soldiers. The frustrated Vietcong eventually brought up a heavy mortar and started a relentless bombardment in their attempts to take the camp. At the same time, they mounted another attack on the perimeter defenses, but they were being held off by the South Vietnamese defenders.

Two Special Forces sergeants decided that the mortar had to be put out of action. In a daring search of the jungle, completely surrounded by the enemy, they eventually managed to locate it and destroy both it and its entire crew. With their mortar out of action, and the knowledge that there was someone prowling around among them, the enemy broke off their attack once again.

Unfortunately, one of the final rounds fired by the mortar had destroyed the camp's generators and there was no hope of repairing them. Under normal circumstances this would not have been too great a problem, but on this occasion a surgeon was in the middle of a delicate operation on a wounded Vietnamese soldier.

At that time, Lieutenant Colonel Burl Campbell was flying his Shadow about five hundred feet above the jungle canopy; he was looking for any "target of opportunity" when he received a call for help and immediately broke off his random search and asked his navigator for a course to the camp.

As he neared the camp, Colonel Campbell talked to the Special Forces commander, who explained the situation and also the fact that the enemy was still in the area and firing spasmodically. Once over the camp, Campbell called his illuminator operator, Staff Sergeant Robert Johnson, and ordered him to turn on the one-million-candlepower light.

As the lumbering Shadow rolled gently into a left orbit, the eerie white beam pierced the darkness and fell on the camp. Campbell identified the operating table and set his sights on it. He knew that in order to give the harried surgeon maximum continuous light he would have to hold the gunship in a tightly controlled orbit.

He disregarded all thoughts of enemy gunfire—for which he was a perfect target—and concentrated his attention on his gunsight and the surgeon below. Although the surgeon was working as fast as he could to save his patient's life, the operation took considerably more time than expected, due to various surgical complications. Forty minutes after the illuminator was turned on, the operation was completed.

When Campbell finally received the signal that the operation was over, and that it had been a success, he was greatly relieved. As he brought the Shadow back to straight and level flight, he discovered that he was soaked with sweat, and so were the members of his crew, as during the entire time orbiting the camp they had been waiting to hear the sound of enemy bullets tearing through the gunship.

The Shadow went back to hunting in the clammy night air and the 71st Squadron added a "save" to its list of kills.

9

AIRCRAFT OF THE MODERN AIR COMMANDO

AC-130
Although previously described in chapter 7, the presentday AC-130 gunship is somewhat different from the earlier models and requires further explanation.

Called the Spectre since the latter days of the Vietnam War, it is a much more potent weapon than the original version, due to the addition of modern equipment and an improved armament system.

Larger engines give it more speed—in excess of three hundred miles per hour—and an air-to-air refueling capability permits it to respond to a call for assistance anywhere in the world without having to land for fuel. The Spectre holds the world record for the longest flight by any C-130–type aircraft, an air time of 29.7 hours.

Armament now consists of two modified 20-mm Vulcan cannons, mounted ahead of and below the leading edge of the wing, each of which can fire 2,500 rounds per minute; one 40-mm Bofors cannon (originally a Navy shipyard gun), mounted below the trailing edge of the wing, that can fire up to 115 rounds per minute. Finally, a real field-artillery piece, a 105-mm Army howitzer, is mounted alongside the Bofors gun and can deliver its bomblike rounds at the rate of 4 per minute.

The Spectre is equipped with advanced global inertial navigation and radar equipment, and infrared and low-light-level television (nighttime) detection systems and sensors. It has a computerized target-acquisition and fire-control system, and both sophisticated electronic and conventional anti-aircraft missile defense systems. It also has a powerful searchlight and a flare-dispensing unit.

The Spectre, as its name suggests, is primarily a nocturnal creature, but it is not limited to nighttime use. It can perform a variety of combat roles, including interdiction, close air support, armed reconnaissance, air-base defense, and forward air controlling under most environmental conditions. During peacetime, because of its incredible sensor and detection systems, the Spectre has been used extensively for search-and-rescue missions in all types of weather, both day and night.

Under normal conditions the Spectre gunship is manned by five officers and nine enlisted personnel, and it is on active duty only with the 16th Special Operations Squadron of the 1st Special Operations Wing.

MC-130

Nicknamed the Black Bird, simply because it is painted all black, but called the Combat Talon, this is a highly modified C-130E used for special-operations activities. Like its companion-in-arms, this craft is equipped with an air-to-air refueling system, which permits long and extended operations.

The Combat Talon is generally unarmed and is a workhorse for unconventional warfare missions. It is equipped with specialized high- and low-speed aerial delivery and resupply equipment utilizing advanced radar and computers, secure communications and data-processing systems, highly sophisticated navigation systems, electronic-warfare equipment, and various types of psychological-warfare equipment.

The Talon is perhaps best known for its ability to snatch downed pilots and crewmen, from either land or water, with the use of the Fulton Surface-to-Air Recovery system (STAR). When a downed aviator is located, the Talon will drop two small packages as close as possible to him. These packages contain the recovery kit, which consists of a heavy-duty canvas harness suit, a 525-foot lift line, a balloon, two aluminum modules and helium, and, most important, a set of instructions printed in several languages and illustrated in cartoon form.

The recovery subject puts on the suit, inflates the balloon with helium, and attaches the lift line. As this is happening, the Talon pilot extends the two recovery arms attached to the center of the aircraft's nose. When not in use, these arms are folded back on either side of the nose and resemble a narrow mustache. When they are swept forward into the operating position they form a V-shaped yoke in front of the Talon and look like feelers on the head of an insect.

With the yoke extended, the pilot keeps the Talon's speed at 150 miles per hour and flies about four hundred feet above the ground toward the lift line. The recovery subject sits on the ground and looks toward the oncoming aircraft as the pilot aims for a point between two markers on the lift line.

When the line enters the yoke it slides into the apex, where it is automatically locked in place. The recovery subject is immediately snatched off the ground, with a force that is no greater than the jolt received from a parachute harness when the parachute first deploys. Should the pilot fail to get the line into the center of the yoke, it will not get caught on the wings or in the propellers, because steel deflector cables, called fending lines, run from each side of the nose just behind the yoke, out to the wing tips.

As the rescued man trails behind the Talon, the crew chief in the rear of the aircraft stands on the open ramp and lowers a heavy weight with hooks attached. When the rescue subject catches the line, a hydraulic winch is used to haul him up into the aircraft.

The STAR rescue system can also be used at night, by the addition of two small lights to the lift line. Instead of aiming between two markers, the pilot must now aim between the lights to catch the line; it is a little more difficult to do at night, but it is a highly effective method of recovering individual personnel from behind enemy lines.

Among other attributes, the Combat Talon is famous for its extremely accurate positioning of both supplies and parachutists into small drop zones, both at night and during inclement weather.

All MC-130 Combat Talons in the Air Force inventory are assigned to the 8th Special Operations Squadron (also known as the Black Bird Squadron) of the 1st Special Operations Wing. A significant part of the Black Bird's mission role is the training of personnel from other United States defense forces and those of friendly foreign nations.

HH-53H Pave Low

The HH-53H helicopter is a single-rotor, heavy-lift aircraft with twin turbine engines and a six-man crew. It can carry some thirty-seven passengers or seven tons of cargo and is used primarily for airlift support during special operations in unconventional warfare.

The Pave Low has a top speed of about two hundred miles per hour and is fitted with two jettisonable auxiliary fuel tanks and a retractable air-to-air refueling probe, which obviously gives it considerable operational capability. It is the most sophisticated helicopter in the free world, as it is equipped with terrain-following/terrain-avoidance ground-mapping radar, forward-looking infrared, Dopler-inertial navigation systems, and various other specialized electronic devices. Equipped in this manner, it can operate in adverse weather, both at night and during daylight hours.

The HH-53H is fitted with armor plating and carries

up to three 7.62-mm miniguns or three .50-calibre machine guns for self-protection or suppressive fire support.

This helicopter is assigned only to the 20th Special Operations Squadron (called the Green Hornets), and it is sometimes referred to by the name given to an earlier version of the same basic type—the Jolly Green Giant.

U-1

This versatile helicopter is a variant of the UH-1 aircraft that was used in Vietnam. It is a twin-turbine-engined, single-rotor aircraft, with a top speed of about 150 miles per hour. It has a crew of four and can carry up to eleven passengers or one ton of cargo.

Considered a multirole helicopter, it can be armed with a variety of weapons, from miniguns to rockets, or a mixture of both, and has proven itself to be an excellent small gunship.

It is in service with both the Green Hornets (20th Special Operations Squadron) and a detachment in Panama.

10

CONCEPTS, ISSUES, DEPLOYMENT AND TRAINING OF THE MODERN AIR COMMANDO

The Air Commando was born of need in 1944 and was phased out by the end of 1947. It was revived at the beginning of the Vietnam conflict and by 1973 had expanded to some thirty-one squadrons with over ten thousand personnel and almost six hundred aircraft.

Despite the fact that the Air Commando conclusively proved that its mode of operation was one of the most successful in combating the two major forms of unconventional warfare—that of the insurgent and that of the guerrilla—and despite the fact that both types of warfare were rapidly increasing during the early and mid-seventies, the United States armed forces were drastically reducing almost all of their special-operations capabilities.

The incident that occurred at the American Embassy in Teheran, Iran, in 1979, and the ensuing and obvious impotence of the United States government in its attempts to rectify the situation, finally brought the point home. Our government and our military leaders realized that our conventional armed forces were woefully lacking in their ability to handle the problem. To send them into Iran in a massive retaliatory move would have been successful, but it would have incurred the wrath of more than half the world. It would have been unnecessary force—like using a sledgehammer to break a small cracked pot, when all that was needed was a deftly applied tap in the right place with a tiny hammer. However, it became obvious that although we thought we had the hammer, we did not have the skill to apply the deft tap, and we acutely embarrassed ourselves.

At the time of the Iranian incident, the Air Commando Special Operations Wing was within weeks of being disbanded. Within twenty-four hours of the Iranian crisis, the imminent disbanding had been postponed and a state of limbo developed for a short time.

Finally, Air Force Special Operations started to grow again and a new-numbered Air Force, the 23rd Air Force, was established and assigned to Military Airlift Command on March 1, 1983. The Air Force Combat Rescue forces (Rescue and Recovery Service) and the Special Operations forces, were consolidated to officially become the 23rd Air Force. The reason for these two particular units being grouped together was fairly simple: they both used the same basic airframe for their operational aircraft; consequently, maintenance support management would be much easier within the command structure.

Once the consolidation took place, the Special Operations forces then became the reactivated 2nd Air Division (as it had been in Vietnam) and was headquartered at Hurlburt Field, Florida.

In diagram form, the command structure would be as follows:

MILITARY AIRLIFT COMMAND
|
23RD AIR FORCE
|
COMBAT RESCUE   2ND AIR DIVISION

The 2nd Air Division's mission role, briefly stated, is the organization, planning, and conduct of all aspects of special operations for the United States Air Force, with a particular emphasis on unconventional warfare. This includes intelligence operations and the planning and interface of all Air Force operations with the unconventional-warfare forces of the other armed services.

The geographical area of operational responsibility of the 2nd Air Division is the entire world, although special units assigned to certain areas will be under the immediate control of the relevant theater commander. In order to maintain its worldwide deployment status, the 2nd Air Division participates in combat exercises throughout the world with all branches of our armed services. In particular, the U.S. Army Rangers and Special Forces, Marine Reconnaissance Units, and Navy SEALs.

The principal operational units of the division are as follows:

1st Special Operations Wing, Hurlburt Field, Florida

USAF Special Operations School, Hurlburt Field, Florida

1st Special Operations Squadron, Clark Air Base, Republic of the Philippines

7th Special Operations Squadron, Rhein-Main Air Base, Federal Republic of Germany

Detachment 1, 2nd Air Division, Howard Air Base, Panama

*   *   *

There are presently three reserve units to which the 2nd Air Division functions as the active duty adviser; these are as follows:

919th Special Operations Group, Duke Field, Florida

193rd Special Operations Group, Harrisburg International Airport, Pennsylvania

302nd Special Operations Squadron, Luke Air Force Base, Arizona

The principal operational, or fighting, arm of the 2nd Air Division is the 1st Special Operations Wing. It is commanded by a colonel and has some twenty-eight special-operations aircraft and a staff of about three thousand military and civilian personnel. The wing's motto is "Any Time, Any Place," and it is made up of the following major units, all located at Hurlburt Field, Florida:

8th Special Operations Squadron (MC-130E Combat Talons)

16th Special Operations Squadron (AC-130H Spectre gunships)

20th Special Operations Squadron (HH-53H Pave Low and UH-1N Twin Huey)

Special Operations Combat Control Team

834th Combat Support Group

These units participate in a considerable number of joint-services training exercises on a continuous basis. The exercises include low-level infiltration and exfiltration missions, search-and-rescue operations, direct attacks in assigned areas and on specific types of targets, convoy-escort duties, and close air support for ground forces.

A considerable amount of training and practice is also carried out with the Rangers, Marines, Army Special Forces, and SEALs, as well as with foreign friendly units, such as the British Special Air Service Regiment (SAS).

The mission role of the three squadrons—8th, 16th and 20th—is fairly obvious because they operate aircraft that have a clearly defined purpose. The mission role of the 834th Combat Support Group is to provide total administrative and logistic support for the entire 1st Special Operations Wing, both at their home base in Florida and in operational deployment overseas.

The mission role of the Special Operations Combat Control Team, more usually called the CCT, is not fully understood by most people, including a great number of those who are serving members of the Air Force. This is because of the highly classified nature of the methods they employ to fulfill their mission role demands and the fact that they do not actually fly aircraft. However, in a comparison of elite fighting groups, the Combat Control Team of the 1st Special Operations Wing must be considered unique because it is "elite within an elite."

Their motto is "First There," and it is a motto they deserve, because part of their mission role is to get to an assigned area in enemy-held territory—by land, sea, or air—to prepare the way for the safe arrival of others. Once they arrive at the designated target area, their mission role is as follows: examine prearranged landing sites or drop zones, or select them; establish either runway markers for landing aircraft or zone-identification markers for troop or supply drops; guidance of aircraft into the landing zones or temporary runways; limited defensive operations; identification of targets for gunships and all manner of fighters, bombers, and helicopters; and generally assisting ground forces in the coordination of air operations to meet whatever requirements the ground-force commanders might have.

Entry into the Combat Control Team is on a voluntary basis, and initial recruiting and selection is basically performed at one location only, the Air Force Air Traffic Control School. This is because the first requirement for members of the team is that they are fully qualified air-traffic controllers. Volunteers are sought among those who have the physical capabilities and mental attitude to handle the training they will receive when they have qualified as air-traffic controllers.

Upon qualifying, they are sent to various Army schools to be trained by the Army's specialists in infantry tactics and operations; navigation; day and night combat patrolling in unfamiliar terrain; reconnaissance operations; close-quarter and unarmed combat; infantry weapons and equipment; escape, evasion, and survival techniques; and infantry communications operations. They are trained in normal military parachute operations, and once they have completed the prescribed number of jumps they are trained in some very specialized parachuting techniques.

Advanced parachuting starts with free-fall or delayed-opening practice. Normal military parachuting is referred to as "static line" jumping (the parachute is opened shortly after the jumper leaves the aircraft by a static line attached to the inside of the aircraft). In free-fall jumping, the parachutist makes the decision and pulls a ripcord, or D-ring, to open the parachute at whatever altitude he chooses. Normal delayed-opening parachute training starts with the jumper leaving the aircraft between five thousand and ten thousand feet above the ground; before the parachute is deployed, the jumper is in the free-fall mode. When taught correctly, an individual can steer him- or herself backward and forward across a wide area of sky before opening the parachute, normally at about twenty-five hundred feet. When the training combat controller has learned to free-fall in this manner, he is taught perhaps the most exhilarating of all forms of parachuting—high-altitude jumping.

There are two basic forms of high-altitude jumping,

normally referred to as HA-HO and HA-LO. The first, HA-HO, is High Altitude–High Opening; it is where the jumper, wearing oxygen-breathing equipment and special clothing, exits the aircraft from heights in excess of forty thousand feet and free-falls for only a short distance before deploying his parachute. With a highly maneuverable parachute the jumper can travel considerable distances across the sky—fifty miles or more—before landing in a specified area.

HA-LO means High Altitude–Low Opening; this is where the jumper, again wearing the oxygen equipment and special clothing, exits the aircraft from thirty or forty thousand feet and free-falls right down to one thousand feet before opening the parachute. During the fall he will steer his body for an incredible ride through the atmosphere and arrive over his target area many miles from where he left the aircraft.

The combat controller first learns the techniques of HA-HO and HA-LO without wearing his combat equipment, but he eventually learns to jump carrying over one hundred pounds of equipment.

After the high-altitude parachute training, the combat controller goes to the other extreme—he is taught combat diving. But before he goes underwater he must learn small-boat-handling techniques, particularly rubber-boat handling, in open water, coastal, river, and lake environments, as well as survival at sea. When these techniques have been perfected, he starts diver training; once adequately trained, he is taught how to work from a submarine. During his submarine training he learns how to exit the vessel when it is resting on the sea bed and then make his way to shore. He is also taught how to enter a submarine underwater, even though it is unlikely that he will ever have to enter such a vessel during normal combat operations.

Once the maritime disciplines have been learned, further parachute training takes place—jumping into rivers, lakes, and the sea under simulated combat conditions.

Training in jungle warfare operations and jungle survival then takes place, followed by desert warfare and some cold-weather, or arctic, training.

Combat airfield-construction techniques and operations are taught by engineers, both Army and Air Force. Vehicle training is another phase—from motorcycles to bulldozers, the Combat Control Team member must at least know how to move them.

After some two and a half to three years of training, the new team member has most of the basic skills required, but there are more to be learned, some in specialized courses and others during combined operations and joint-forces exercise.

The Special Operations Combat Control Team is indeed a most elite group, although they are not actually an aggressor or fighting force; they are trained in more military disciplines than most of the special-forces groups in the entire United States armed forces. Because their job is not seek-and-destroy, little has been heard of them, but because of their training and knowledge of special operations they are occasionally used for some very special clandestine operations where they function in a very aggressive manner. For the most part, however, the Combat Control Team does not actively seek contact with the enemy, but in almost every other respect they are to the Air Force what the SEALs are to the Navy and the Special Forces are to the Army.

In October, 1983, the Combat Control Team lived up to its motto when aircraft of the 1st Special Operations Wing arrived at the tiny island nation of Grenada in support of the U.S. Rangers. The team was on the ground when the Rangers landed—they were "First There."

Their colleagues in the other units of the 1st Special Operations Wing were close behind them, and, as the operation commenced, an AC-130 Spectre gunship of the 16th Squadron was the first U.S. aircraft to reply to enemy fire. In doing so, it destroyed a gun position and thus achieved the first air-to-ground "kill" during the recapture of the island. Throughout the entire operation, the modern Air Commando demonstrated their capability in an exemplary manner in the support of the ground forces.

The future of Air Force Special Operations now seems to be assured, as our government and senior military leaders have realized that they are a potent weapon, particularly when used in conjunction with the elite groups of the Army, Navy, and Marines. In the battle against a continuing increase in subversive insurgency, guerrilla warfare, and terrorism, the Special Operations Wing has the men and the equipment to play a decisive role. New equipment and further training will increase the scope and capabilities of the wing and they will be prepared to respond to the threat of various forms of unconventional warfare in defense of our national interests—"Any Time, Any Place."

11

BATTLEFIELD LOG:
Grenada—October, 1983

When the battle order for operation Urgent Fury was called, the 1st Special Operations Wing swung into action. Air crews were summoned hastily for briefings, and ground crews were called to prepare the aircraft; the flight line at Hurlburt Field in Florida was a scene of hectic but orderly activity.

Aircraft were fueled to maximum capacity, and pallets of ammunition—20-mm, 40-mm, and 105-mm—were hauled out to the gunships and offloaded. Guns were checked, electronic equipment and radios were tested; everything possible was given the proverbial onceover.

Onceover applied to simple mechanical items. It did not apply to the maps and charts that were being studied by the pilots and navigators. It did not apply to communications frequencies, call signs, secure codes, holding areas' weather forecasts, refueling rendezvous areas, enemy armament and anti-aircraft defense systems, or a myriad of logistic arrangements.

The Combat Talons were the first to leave, their four huge propellers, driven by almost twenty thousand horsepower, made a continuous slashing sound as they sliced through the dense Florida air. The gunships, already loaded to combat weight—at least ten tons more than their normal maximum payload—were making last-minute adjustments and aligning their guns.

The first gunship called for taxi clearance and seemed to waddle under its heavy load as it made its way to the threshold of the takeoff runway. As more of the dull, dark-gray-painted aircraft moved slowly along the taxiways, the pilots could feel the extra weight. The foreboding-looking aircraft were a little slow to respond to steering inputs, almost as if they were reluctant to leave the security of the flight line. They were sluggish in their response to the throttles and had lost the little bouncing and shaking movements they usually had when they traveled over slight undulations on the taxiways. When the pilots eased back on the throttles, they slowed down very quickly but seemed reluctant to stop.

During the takeoff, the engine noises were different, and it took considerably more runway before the chubby aircraft became airborne. Once in the air, things seemed to get a little better, but response to the controls was markedly different.

To the crews of the gunships, familiar, friendly noises and sounds seemed to be either magnified or different in some way; all movements appeared to be stilted—not quite slow motion, but definitely slower than normal. Most of the crews assumed that it was because the gunships were so heavily loaded, but some felt that it was a sensation caused by the thought of what might lie ahead. This mission was not an exercise—there was going to be shooting, and shooting back. The truth of the matter was that the sensation they felt was a combination of two things—the heavily loaded aircraft, and altered senses. This is common among warriors about to go into battle, particularly unfledged warriors, and is caused by anticipation, concern, doubt, and various other emotions.

Seasoned warriors are not immune to it, as they have both an advantage and a disadvantage in knowing what to expect. There were several pilots and crew members on board both the gunships and the Talons who had fought in Vietnam, and to them it was the same old feeling all over again.

When the Spectre gunships cleared the runway at Hurlburt Field they headed straight for the nearby firing ranges. All the guns had been checked and aligned on the ground, but they now had to be test fired. Although this could have been done somewhere near the actual target area, it was felt that it would be safer to complete the testing and make any final adjustments before setting out on the long journey to the island of Grenada.

With the test firing completed, the Spectres started to head southeast across Florida. Shortly after departing, one of the gunships lost the power in one of its four engines and was forced to turn back to Hurlburt Field. As the aircraft was combat-loaded it was well over its maximum permissible landing weight and was forced to fly south over the Gulf of Mexico and dump most of its fuel.

Meanwhile, back at Hurlburt Field, the ground crews were once again hard at work, only this time at a much faster pace. They brought a spare aircraft to the flightline, ran up the engines, and tested all its systems. It was then loaded with fuel, tons of ammunition, and food and water for the crew. By the time the malfunctioning gunship landed, the relief craft was ready and waiting for them.

Shortly after landing their three-engined gunship, the pilot and crew were back in the air in the spare aircraft, familiarizing themselves with another set of strange noises and trying to settle in for the long journey.

The leading gunships were far out over the ocean by the time the spare craft was airborne. There was no possibility of the spare catching up with them, but it had managed to get airborne with sufficient time left to reach the island just as dawn was breaking. As the first assault on the island was planned to commence during the closing minutes of the predawn period, there was every likelihood that they would not miss much action.

Throughout the night the Talons and Spectres droned on toward the island, and in the early hours of the morning the Talons were the first to make contact with the aerial tankers. Slowly and steadily each Talon flew up under the tail of the giant tankers, and the refueling boom was carefully lowered from the rear of the tanker and stabbed into the receptacle above the cockpit on the Talon. When all the Talons were completely refueled, they continued on to their holding area southwest of Grenada.

The thirsty gunships made their rendezvous with another fleet of aerial tankers, refueled, and then pulled away to their designated holding area.

As the Talons and Spectres waited for the aircraft carrying the U.S. Rangers to arrive, the weather started to get worse as a storm front was moving through the area. The meteorologists assured them that the front would pass through before the assault was to take place, but that was no consolation to the crews of the Spectres and Talons—particularly the Talons, who were sitting at an altitude where the heaviest part of the front would pass. Under normal circumstances it would not have been a problem; they would have simply changed altitudes to avoid the weather. However, what concerned the Talon pilots was the fact that the special role they had to play, during the actual invasion of the island, required them to fly a precise pattern at a specific altitude in a definite area. The problem was that they were already established in their area and could not move out of it without jeopardizing the entire operation.

Another annoying fact was that although the storm front would be well clear of the island before the invasion began, the Talons would still be in it, thereby making their job even more difficult. Contrary to all their training, and all the normal rules of airmanship, the Talons were simply going to have to hold their positions, perform their vital function, and take whatever punishment the storm dealt them.

The Spectre pilots were in the same storm and were in a similar situation to that of the Talon pilots because they could not move out of the area until the invasion actually began. The reason for this was the fact that a fleet of troopships carrying the Rangers, and their high-speed fighter escorts, was moving toward the island. There were also various other aircraft involved in the operation that were assigned to nearby areas, and there was a defensive system established to cope with any possible outside threat. Because of these factors, all aircraft had to remain in their assigned territories until the time came for them to perform their functions in the mission.

As dawn approached, the first Spectres moved toward the oncoming troopships to lead them to the Point Salinas airfield on the south side of the island.

The plan of action called for the first troopship to land hard and fast just before first light. The first wave of Rangers and the Combat Control Team members would come out of the aircraft firing. As the Rangers moved away from the aircraft, the Combat Control Team members would make sure that the empty troopship was taxied off the runway onto safe ground. As this was going on, the second troopship was supposed to be touching down and coming to a halt with Rangers charging out of it. The airfield would now be under the management of the Combat Control Team, which intended to bring the laden troopships onto the ground at the rate of at least one every fifteen to twenty seconds.

The Combat Control Team members had studied every available map and photograph of the airfield, and they had every available detail of the runway and the immediate area firmly implanted in their minds. They would be landing with the fast-moving Rangers, whom they had worked and trained with on many previous occasions, and they knew that they could rely on them to provide adequate protection.

The first Spectre moved ahead of the lead troopship as it started its long approach for a landing. The sensors in the Spectre sent their invisible beams probing out through the darkness to scan the airfield below; they could detect no enemy movement. Apart from a twenty-knot crosswind, caused by the storm front that had just gone through, everything appeared to be going as planned.

Moments later, out of a maze of electronic signals that were being fed through the Spectres' computers came a signal that suggested something was wrong. The sensor operators quickly checked their system and received positive identification of "trash" on the runway ahead. Seconds later, they knew the trash was a series of obstructions that had obviously been placed on the runway to deter a landing.

The information was quickly relayed to the landing-force commander, who immediately made the decision that his Rangers would change from an air-landing mode to an air-drop mode. The leading troopship was immediately informed and he pulled off his approach run; all the other troopships were instructed to follow him.

The Talon crews, faithfully holding their station in the storm front, "saw" the troopships pull away from the island and knew immediately that something was wrong. A few minutes later, they were informed that the assault was delayed—not aborted—and they were requested to continue holding their station.

On board the troopships the pilots were experiencing "minor turbulence." It was not caused by weather conditions, but by scores of Rangers frantically moving around inside the aircraft in their efforts to get their parachutes on and to rearrange their equipment for an air drop. The Combat Control Team had the same problem, as they now had to reorganize their special equipment to ensure that it would not get damaged on landing.

Within fifteen minutes the Rangers and Combat Control Team members were ready for the jump, and they were informed that they would be going in from five hundred feet—the lowest possible height for a parachute drop. It was a decision that had been made by the Ranger commander after he had been informed by the lead Spectre that it had "sensed" heavy anti-aircraft gun positions at about the nine-hundred-foot level on the hills adjoining the airfield. The experienced Ranger commander knew that antiaircraft guns are not designed to fire downward, and although a standard operational jump was normally done at one thousand feet he had the authority to bring it down to five hundred feet. He did not like the idea of losing scores of men if an aircraft was to be shot down.

The leading formation of troopships dropped to five hundred feet and swung back toward the airfield. As this was taking place, the Spectres moved into a covering position over the airfield and waited for the first sign of enemy gunfire.

Anti-aircraft guns opened up as soon as the troopships arrived and a hail of flak exploded in the skies. There were a few guns down by the airfield, but they had their shellbursts set too high; nevertheless, they were an immediate danger and had to be taken out. The guns on the hilltop started firing, but the Ranger commander had been right—they could not depress low enough to hit the aircraft down at five hundred feet. The lower guns did not seem capable of traversing fast enough as the troopships emptied their bellies of Combat Control Team members and Rangers. The sky was pockmarked with bursting flak as the Spectres went into action against the guns. The first "kill" came when one gun fell to the withering fire of a Spectre's 20-mm Vulcan cannon.

The troopships were now dropping Rangers at a fast rate and the twenty-knot wind was catching the billowing parachutes and spreading them around the airfield. Because of this, the Spectres could not take the chance of shooting too close to the runway—there was always the possibility that a parachute would drift into their line of fire. However, the enemy had exposed themselves in several other positions and were firing at the troopships that were dropping the remainder of Rangers and at the Rangers who were already on the ground. Their fire on the Rangers did not last long, as they were dealt a shattering blow when a Spectre effectively "hosed" them down with 20-mm and 40-mm fire.

When the Combat Control Team and the Rangers were firmly established on the airfield, they called the Spectres in to silence four well-hidden enemy guns, one of which was located in a building overlooking the airfield. The building received a long burst from the 40-mm Bofors gun and the remaining positions were dealt with by 20-mm Vulcan fire. Shortly afterward, all resistance at Point Salinas airport was wiped out.

The spare gunship ("Spare") finally arrived over the island and was soon at work, seeking out pockets of enemy resistance. As the Rangers started to move off the airfield they had the constant support of the gunships, and well-entrenched enemy gun positions that had held their fire when the soldiers were on the airfield now exposed themselves and were quickly silenced.

On their way out of the airfield one group of Rangers was being pinned down by fire that was coming from one house in the middle of a terrace of four. They called for help and Spare came to assist them. They identified the building for the late-arriving gunship, and its pilot released one delayed-firing round from the 105-mm howitzer. The shell went straight through the roof and exploded in the basement. Moments later, enemy soldiers were seen running out of the house with a white flag held high above their heads.

Some time later, Spare was prowling around when three armored personnel carriers were spotted moving down a road toward a group of Rangers. The Rangers were engaged in a particularly fierce firefight with a group of enemy soldiers and were in danger of being outgunned if the personnel carriers got much farther along the road.

Spare called a warning to the Rangers, as the armored vehicles were a little too close for gunship fire without some direction from the ground forces. The Rangers' reply was short—they wanted the gunship to take care of the problem, immediately.

The armored personnel carriers were a little distance apart from one another on the narrow road. The pilot picked the rear vehicle first, aligned the gunsight, and squeezed the firing button for the 105-mm howitzer. The gun made a coughlike, barking sound, followed by a noise that resembled an unfinished whistle as the shell left the barrel. As the hydraulic recoil mechanism absorbed the shock of the propelling charge, the shell slammed into the ground some fifteen feet away from the armored vehicle, showering it with dirt and pushing it to one side. Ten seconds later the howitzer was ready to fire again and the pilot squeezed the firing button. This time the projectile slammed straight through the top of the vehicle and wrecked it. The noise of the aircraft's engines was not loud enough to drown out the cheers of the crew at their first vehicle "kill."

The pilot lined up on the second vehicle and the howitzer responded instantly when he touched the firing button. The result was the same as before—the round went straight through the top of the armored personnel carrier and destroyed it. The driver of the remaining personnel carrier was just starting to move his vehicle out of the way when the next round from the flying artillery piece found its mark and unerringly slammed straight through the top of it.

It did not take the enemy very long to guess that the Rangers would attempt to rescue the American medical students at the Grand Anse Campus of the Saint George's

Medical College. As the Rangers moved toward the campus, the enemy placed a defensive ring of troops around it. On the roofs of two nearby hotels, the Spice Island and the Grenada Beach, they set up heavy gun emplacements that would give them a direct line of fire onto any helicopter that attempted to reach the campus. The rescue attempt came at 1630 hours, and two Spectres took care of the hotels—destroying them in a fifteen-minute display of incredibly accurate gunfire.

The British Governor General, Sir Paul Scoon, was a prisoner in his own mansion, which was surrounded by enemy troops and light armor. When a SEAL rescue team managed to get into the house, the enemy decided to attack, and the SEALs called for a gunship.

Spare arrived on the scene within minutes and, at the request of the SEAL team leader, engaged in a remarkable display of accuracy and controlled firepower by "walking" a ring of 20-mm and 40-mm rounds right up to the walls of the house. As a result, the enemy retreated and the governer general was flown to safety.

The Spectre gunships roamed the southern part of the island of Grenada for the next two days in support of the Rangers and of the Army's 82nd Airborne division. During that time they were called upon again and again, day and night, to wipe out enemy gun emplacements and pockets of fierce resistance. On October 27, they were called upon by the 82nd Airborne to assist in the taking of the Cuban Headquarters, Calvigny Barracks. By the time the Spectres had finished hosing down the fortresslike structure with 20-mm, 40-mm, and 105-mm shells, the enemy had given up and the 82nd Airborne had simply to walk in to take over.

When Urgent Fury was over, the aircraft and men of the 1st Special Operations Wing of the United States Air Force —the modern Air Commando—headed home. They had just played one of the major roles in the first war that the United States had won in thirty-eight years, and they had demonstrated their right to be called an elite fighting force.

ABOUT THE AUTHOR

IAN PADDEN was born and educated in England. During service with the British Military he learned to fly and also developed an interest in specialized reconnaissance, espionage, and counter insurgency warfare. His interests in these subjects required him to have a thorough knowledge of other special ("elite") military units throughout the world.

He was taught deep-sea diving by Royal Navy instructors and worked as a commerical diver in construction, salvage, and offshore oil drilling. He spent further time in the oil industry working as a driller, drilling supervisor, and drilling engineer and was later employed by one of the world's leading subsea drilling equipment manufacturers as a specialist engineer and training instructor. He left the company to become a drilling consultant, and in that capacity has been responsible for drilling oil wells, both on land and offshore, throughout the world.

One of Ian's hobbies is aerobatic competition flying. He has been a member of the British Aerobatic Team since 1978 and has represented Great Britain in two world championships.

Ian Padden began writing in 1963 when he presented a special paper on "The Foundation, Formation and Operating Principles of the Roman Army" to the British Army School of Education. In 1965 he assisted in the writing of "The Principles of Diving" by Mark Terrell (Stanley Paul: London). During his career in the oil industry, he was commissioned to write training manuals and narrations for training films. He has also written two television scripts and various treatments for documentaries. He is currently finishing a full-length novel.